Joycesqueanisms: 1

JOYCESQUEANISMS:
the wit and wisdom of André Joyce

by Michael Joseph Halm

Joycesqueanisms: 2

Since Joycesque and Joycean had already been used for the creative literature of James Joyce, Joycesquean was coined to describe that of André Joyce. He is best known for having coined "googology" for the art and science of large numbers and "ibibious", a djective describing the acronym, "I believe I believe it". The following are other samples of his vocabulary collected by his students and relatives.

a-invariant: describing a word beginning with the letter a and without another one
A-keili: [Fin.] describes words with only a as a vowel: banana, bandana, mama, papa, ta-ta
aagram: [anagram with second letter deleted] word formed from another by deletion of second letter and transposition: dream = dame = Edam = made = mead
aagram string: string made from aagrams: dream + mead + dam = dreameadam
aangram: [anagram with second and third letters exchanged] (132, 1324, 4321, 13245, 13254, 43215, 43251, 53214, 53241, etc.) anagrams: satin = stain
aapa: ["ad astra per aspera" acronym] to the stars through troubles
aatiborh: [George Moore acronym] "After all there is but one race, humanity."
ababa: [Sanskrit] ten-to-the-seventy-seventh, seventy-sevenplex = 10^{77}
abacupus: [back-up abacus portmanteau] abacus to back up the abacus to back up the calculator
abback: [affrount antonym] insulting someone behind their back
abbuda: [Sanskrit] ten-to-the-fifty-sixth, fifty-sixplex = 10^{56}
abbreathiated: [abbreviated + breath portmanteau] short-winded, nearly out of breath
abbreeziated: [abbreviated + breeze portmanteau] like short gust of wind
abbrhyme: [abbr. + rhyme portmanteau, Willard R. Espy's abbreviated rhyme] synthetic rhyme using abbreviation: "A Mrs. kr. Mr., then how her Mr. kr. He kr., kr., kr., until he raised a blr."
Abilene paradox: People can make decisions based not on what they actually want to do, but on what they think that other people want to do, with the result that everybody decides to do something that nobody really wants to do
absurditty: [absurd + ditty portmanteau] nonsense song
abecdarius: alphabetical acrostic like Pss 25, 34
abracada brat: [abracadabra + brat portmanteau] mischievous child that can disappear in an instant
abracadaver: [abracadaba cadaver portmanteau] dead body that miraculously revives
abtciop: [Aesop acronym] "A bad temper carries its own punishment."
acalmghaw: [Franklin acronym] "After crosses and losses, men grow humbler and wiser."
accrimatize: [acclimatize + crime portmanteau] become accustomed to crime as both police and criminals do
acephalous: refers to word without first letter, line without first word, poem without first line
acrograms: words that share the same initial letter
acronym: word from initials of other words: BIBLE: Basic Instructions Before Leaving Earth; BRAIN: Box Retaining Any Ideas Needed, Biological Receptacle for Assorted Ideas and Notions; EVITA: Endless Vivacity In The Argentine; IChThYS: Jesus Christ Son of god [Greek]; JAWS: Just A White Shark; SHERLOCK HOLMES: Sleuth's Habitually Elementary Reasoning Left Organized Crime Kingless. He's Overwhelmed Literate Masses Ever Since; SHOVEL: Sharp Hand-Operated Vertical Earth Lifter; SNAIL: Slimy Night Animal Invading Lettuces; THE SOUND OF MUSIC: This Has Everything: Syrupy Outbursts, Uplifting Nannies, Dancing Over Flowery Mounds, Unctuous Songs Involving Children

acronym, recursive: [Douglas Hofstadter] self-referential acronym in which the initial letter stands for the word itself, GOD = G(OD) O(ver)D(jinn) = GODOD = G(OD) O(ver) D(jinn) O(ver) D(jinn) = GODODOD, etc.

acrostic: acronymous poem, like Pss. 9, 10, 25, 34, 37, 111, 112, 119,145, includes initial, middle (mesostich), progressive and final(telestic), see abecedarius

acrosstic: [across + acrostic portmanteau, Poe] acrostic variation in which nth letter in nth line is significant

acu-puncture: [acupuncture hyphenym] precision deflation

acuestics: [acoustics + cue sticks portmanteau] sound of sticks striking balls or balls striking other balls on pool or billiard table

ad antiquitatem: fallacy of appealing to tradition

ad baculum: fallacy of appeal to fear

ad crumenam: fallacy of appeal to wealth

ad hominem: fallacy of arguing against arguser not argument

ad ignorantiam: fallacy of not knowing any better

ad lapidem: fallacy of assuming absurdity

ad nauseam: fallacy of repetition until opposition gives in

ad novitatem: fallacy of appeal to newest fad

ad numerum: fallacy of appeal to larger number of people

ad verecundiamad: fallacy of appeak to authority

adad: [aut disce aut discede acronym] learn or leave

adam ant: [adamant mondegreen] first male drone born from first queen ant

addamint: [adamant mondegreen] increase breath freshener

admirable: [admiral + -able compound] worthy of promotion to the rank of admiral

adromedary: [apothecary + dromedary portmanteau] camel carrying hospital supplies

Ade's Law: Anyone can win, unless there's a second entry.

æquicalculus: Roman numerology, like Ionians' isopsephia or Hebrews' gematria

aeious: [back-formation from Dmitri A. Borgman's aeiou word] describes word with 5 vowels: abstemious, dialogue, equation, sequoia

aesat: [Aesop acronym] "Any excuse'll serve a tyrant."

Af Jinni: describes words which change to another word when a double vowel with a consonant between changes to another when reduced to the vowel, see Bagari, ..., Zagari

afoofa: [Dumas acronym palindrome] "All for one, one for all."

after-math: [aftermath mondegreen] relief and/or exhaustion following calculations

afahmasp: [acronym] "A fool and his money are soon parted."

afaik: [acronym] as far as I know

affaplectic: [affable + apoplectic portmanteau] prone to outbursts of good humor

affirming the consequent: fallacy of implying that if p then q and q are true then p is, CKCpqqp

afordable: [affordable mondegreen] able to by a Ford automobile

afrodesiac: [afro- + aphrodesiac portmanteau] African love charm or potion

afterclap: [paleologism] unexpected damaging or unsettling event following a supposedly closed affair

agenarian: [nonagenarian hyphenym back-formation] person under 90 or over 99

agamemnonym: [Edward R. Wolpow's Agamemnon word] word with three or more palindromic trigrams

aglisiah: [William Makepeace Thackeray acronym] "A good laugh is sunshine in a home."

aglitor: [Thomas Fuller acronym] "A good life is the only religion."

agmenonym: [Agamemnon back-formation + -nym] word transformed into agamemnonym by adding appropriate letter after bigrams to form palindromic trigrams

agonist: [ant-/protaganist back-formation] main character whether hero/ine, villain/ess or anti-hero/ine
agulate: [coagulate back-formation] someone agulating by themselves
ahmtnwog: [Pope acronym] "An honest man's the noblest work of God."
ahtihhsih: [Prv 23:7 acronym] "As he thinketh in his heart, so is he."
aibohphobiac: [mynynym back-formation] person with abnormal fear of palindromes
aibohpphobiac: [mynynym back-formation] person with abnormal fear of palinddromes, "double-yolked" palindromes
ailihphilia: [Dr. Otto Rotcod] abnormal love of palindromes
ainamaniac: [mynynym back-formation] person with abnormal desire for palindromes
aip: [ab love principium] start with the most important
AIQ: [AI + IQ portmanteau acronym] measurement of "artificial intelligence" as in the results of a Turing test
air-headed: [airhead hyphenym] describing a word beginning with air- but not related to air: airedale
airborn: [curtailed airborne] born while in midflight
aircraft: [mondegreen] art of making things out of air (usually with the aid of balloons)
airudite: [air + erudite portmanteau] sounding good, but full of hot air
ajstaj: [acronym] "A joy shared's twice a joy."
akkhobini: [Sanskrit] ten-to-the-forty-second, forty-twoplex, 10^{42}
alindrome: [beheaded palindrome] near-palindrome that lacks initial letter
Alan's Law: The theory is supported as long as the funds are.
albanecktross: [albatross around neck wordle] burden
Aldhelmian: like Aldhelm, saintly Anglo-Latin riddlemaster (c. 640-709)
alejandrino: [Sp.] 7+7-syllabled stich
alexandrine: 12-syllabled verse, usually iambic hexameter
alfimftaif: [Molière acronym] "A learned fool is more foolish than an ignorant fool."
algaerhythm: [algae + algorithm portmanteau] undulating movement of sea plant
Algoreism: [Al Gore + algorism portmanteau] quotation unique to Al Gore
alicoric: [a- + licorice portmanteu] jellybeans with the black licorice ones removed
aliennation: country overrun with invading extraterrestrials
alladt: [acronym] "A little learning's a dangerous thing."
Allah cart: wheelbarrow used for transporting sacred Moslem objects
alleaveate: [alleviate + leave portmanteau] what trees and rakers do in the Fall
allegater: someone who makes allegations
Allen's Law: [Agnes Allen] Almost anything's easier to get into than out of.
alliteration: with initial consonant rhyme: eighty-eight, ninety-nine, sixty/seventy-six/seven, thirty-three thousand thirty-three, twenty-two twenty-two
alliterature: [alliterative literature portmanteau] work emphasizing alliteration: "The Siege of Belgrade" by Alaric Alexander Watts
allonym: name already used by someone else, like "Dionysius" by Pseudo-Dionysius
alltruist: [all + altruist portmanteau] believer is All-Good
alphabent: sentence with alphabetical acronym: "A brilliant Chinese doctor exhorted four graduating hospital interns: ' Just keep looking, men: no other prescription quickly relieves sore throats, unless veterinarians x-ray your zebras.'" ("Mona Lisa"), "A bee, collecting dewy emanations from gladioli, homed in jerkily, knocking lumpy, misshapen nodes on particularly queer-looking roses, showering the underlying vegetation with xanthic (yellow) zygospores.",

"A born coward, Darius eventually found great happiness in judicially kicking loud-mouthed nepotists openly picking quarrels, rightly saying that unkindness vitiated warring Xerxes' youthful zeal.", "A brilliant Cockney doctor emerged from Gynaecology, having incautiously just knocked long-suffering matron's neurologist out: protesting (quite rightly so) that untrained veterinarians wouldn't've x-rayed your zygoma.", "As birds can dive even from great heights, I just know larks must nest on pinnacles, quietly recollecting shattered thoughts, until violent winds xenomorphosize yon zones.", (5 by Graham Parlett)

alphabet

alphabettor: A for ism [aphorism], B for pork [beef or pork], C foryourself [see for yourself], …

alphabit: [alphabet bit] alphabet transformation rebus: abcdfghijkltnopqrstuvwxyz = cut e cute, abcdefhijkltnopqrstuvwxyz = g out = gout, abcdefghijkltnopqrstuvwxyz = for m a t = format, abcdefghijkmnopqrstuvwxyz = no l = noel, abcdfghijklmnopqrtuvwxyz = no s, e = nose, abcdefghijklmnopqrstuvwxzy - shift y = shifty

alphacrashing: describing word(s) with letter(s) in same position as in alphabet: <u>A bad egg</u> <u>hit</u> the wi<u>pers</u> two <u>ways</u>.

alphadecimal: aka base thirty-six, symbolized by ten digits and twenty-six letters of alphabet, n_{36}

alphal: [alphabetical contraction] with same vowels in alphabetical order, see betical

alphamagic square: magic square in which number of letters in number names is also magic

five	twenty-two	eighteen
twenty-eight	fifteen	two
twelve	eight	twenty-five

alphametic: cryptarithmetic with meaningful words

alphatrip: geographical word chain: Alcatraz, Zurich, Hamburg, Grenada

alphawords: pangrammic crossword: (across) jove, plights, zany; (down)mobs, quick, dwarf, pyx

alphome: [Susan Thorpe, "alph(a) + ome(ga)"] alphabetical anagram: aegilops: a species of oak tree or an eye ulcer, beefily, billowy

also-ran: [mondegreen] children guilty by association with the one who broke the window

altar ego: self-centered priest or server

alternade: word that can be broken into smaller alternate-letter words: see barbarianism, binade, trinade, quadrade, quintade, strike-out

alter native: [alternative mondegreen] change indigenous population's customs
altohumorous: [altocumulus cloud + humorous portmanteau] describes clown with high squeaky voice
alwaysthemore: antonym of nevertheless
amalgam: [Susan Thorpe] anagram from two smaller words or phrases: "saint" + "devil" = "invalid set", "Nureyev" + "Salome" = "Some envy alure."
Amagran: [anagram Davrosism] Spoonerism-like secret language that swaps initial and final consonants
amapah: [Emerson acronym] "All men are poets at heart."
Amara's law: [Roy Amara] We tend to overestimate the effect of a technology in the short run and underestimate the effect in the long run.
ambigation: [4 : 3/2 :: tetration : ?] operation combining addition, multiplication, exponentiation and tetration as with $2 + 2 = 2x2 = 2^2 = {}^22 = 4$
ambinym: word with multiple meaning, including antonyms
ambidexter: [paleologism] middleman who plays both sides against each other
amealuate: [aleliorate + meal portmanteau] eat desert to makeup for not-so-good meal
amhmacc: [acronym] "A merry heart makes a cheery countenance."
amicable: [Pythagoras' "friendly"] with divisors which add to a number whose divisors add to itself
Amish: [Percy Moore Manx + -ish] describing poem form variation with final two lines left unwritten and reversed
amlal: [Emerson acronym] "All mankind loves a lover."
ammsybav: [Aesop acronym] "A man may smile, yet be a villain."
amociafuf: [Cicero acronym] "A man of courage is also full of faith."
amoebean: with alternating speakers
ampa: ["Ad multos annos prosperos!" (To many prosperous years!) acronym] live long and prosper
amphiboly: ambiguous sentence
amphigorical: almost making sense
amphinym: ambiguous words that can be taken to mean quite different things: cleave (split or cling), dust (sprinkle with or cleaned of), fast (moving or motionless), nowhere (no where or now here), seeded (with or without seeds), shelled (with or without shells), superbowl (super bowl or superb owl), weeknights (week nights or wee knights)
amphisbaena: word which when cut can becomes two new words: addiction, anarch, ashore, asphalt, asset, automat, automobile, breakage, caprise, capsize, carat, carpet, cartridge, category, comfortable, convention, cornice, current, curtail, dietitian, disclose, donkey, donor, door, dovetail, expose, fanfare, farrow, forties, fortune, history, humbug, impunity, improve, increase, infirm, inform, invest, issue, lawfully, legally, lonesome, mandate, manor, marten, mattress, meat, mission, mistrust, mummy, napkin, ontogenesis, onus, padlock, panties, pardon, partake, penally, pigeon, plangent, plumage, plummet, portion, primate, procession, quicksand, ruefully, rummy, rumpus, sinus, slither, soapstone, softsoap, sodden, target, toaster, totally, whimper, written
amphisbaena, tied: amphisbaena which when cut becomes two new words the tail of one being the head of the other: archives, asset, ballast, carpet, castile, centime, comfortable, cornice, curtail, disclose, donor, ductile, forties, fortune, legal, madam, manor, marten, mastiff, missing, mistake, mistrust, panties, partake, pastime, planet, plumage, primate, rampage, sorties, straighten, tartar, violate, wanton, whiskey

anacrostic: combination acronym and multiple anagrams

anachronym: [anachronistic acronym portmanteau] paleologistic acronym

anaglyph: three-dimensional verbal text

anagram: word(s) formed from letters of a given word or phrase: satyros = Sa Tyros. new door = one word, Blame Mabel. Texas taxes, The Beatles = these bleat

anagrammar: [Christopher McManus] kind of word chain with variable links

analphabetical: aka zeewyexical, zyxical, refers to reverse Roman alphabet, but also to other alphabets, such as, Hawaiian (wuponmlkihea)

analysandum: term analyzed

analysans: terms of analysis

anany: [curtailed ananym] describing transdeletion in which word is reversed and final letter deleted: anany(petal) = late

ananum: [ananym back-formation] number's reverse, R(n)

ananym: aka drow, reversagram, semordnilap, word reversed: desserts (stressed), deliver (reviled), recaps (spacer)

anaphora: initial repetition in secession: "I came; I saw; I conquered."

anapocryphal: [ana- + apocryphal compound] authentic, true

anarithmonym: [ananym + arithmonym portmantmanteau] reversed number name, beginning at three hundred (derdnuh eerht)

anarhope: opposite of a rhope, decreasing in size letter by letter

anastrophe: inversion of words or syntagms: "Came the dawn."

anatonym: [anatomy + -nym] body part name used as verb: elbow, eye, finger, foot, hand, head, mouth, nose, tail, thumb; or technical body part name: areola (nipple area), canthus (where eyelids meet), coccyx (tail bone), coxa (hip bone), diaphysis (bone shaft), dorsum (top of tongue), epiphysis (bone head), fovea (blind spot on retina), frenulum (thin muscle under tongue), hallux (big toe), ischium (back of hip bone), maxilla (upper mouth bone), nasopharynx (passage between nose and throat), opisthenar (back of hand), oropharynx (passage between mouth and throat), patella (kneecap), phalanx (finger or toe bone), philtrum (indentation between nose and upper lip), pinna (external ear), pollex (thumb), popliteal (hollow in back of knee), pubis (front of hip bone), sclera (white of eye), thenar (fleshy pad below thumb), tragus (fleshy bump between face and ear cavity), vomer (slender bone between nostrils

anatonum: body part that designates a number in counting: fingers, toes, nose, etc.

andagram: [and + anagram portmanteau] transadditional anagram from original word and one extra letter: piecrust + r = scripture

Anderson's Law: "Any system or program, however complicated, if looked at in exactly the right way, will become even more complicated."

angelic: [Matthew Fox] with infinite number of terminating zeros, multiple of surreal number ten-to-infinity, $10^{00}n$

angram: transdeletion with third letter deleted and rest moved

Anguish: [anguished + English portmanteau] homonymous, ambiguous English, particularly hastily written headlines: "Police discover crack in Australia", "Tuna biting off Washington coast", "Traffic dead rise slowly", "Collegians are turning to vegetables", "Milk drinkers are turning to powder", "Caribbean islands drift to left", "Local man has longest horns in Texas", "Dealers will hear car talk Friday noon", "Enraged cow injures farmer with ax", "Two Soviet ships collide, one dies"

animateur: [French] person respected for communicating difficult, technical concepts in easily understood, commonplace language

animultitude: term of venery: troop of baboons, cete of badgers, se(dge of bitterns, sounder of boars, bellowing of bullfinches, drove of bullocks, clowder of cats, clutch of chickens, gulp of cormorants, covert of coots, bask of crocs, murder of crows, cowardice of curs, pod of dolphins, pitying of doves, bed of eels, busyness of ferrets, skulk of foxes, gaggle of geese, tower of giraffes, rasp of guinea fowl, bloat of hippos, lepe of leopards, pride/sawt of lions, plague of locusts, sord of mallards, richnesse of martens, parliament of owls, nide/nye of pheasants, passel of possums, gaze of raccoons, mischief of rats, unkindness of ravens, crash of rhinos, squabble of seagulls, shivver of sharks, dray of squirrels, gam of whales, wisdom of wombats, descent of woodpeckers, dazzle of zebras

anonski: [paleologism] later

anpsi: [animal psi portmanteau] paranormal powers of animals

answerve: [answer swerve portmanteau] answer with a tangential redirection

antanaclasis: using a word twice, with two different meanings

ante-Etna: [mynynym] before last eruption of Mt. Etna

anteek: [antique + eek portmanteau] anything that hasn't been used so far beyond its use-by date that it's frightening

anterhyme: initial rhyme

anthropomorphism: fallacy of attributing humanity to animals

anti-dote: [antidote hyphenym] show no favoritism at all

anti-frieze: [frieze antonym] against wall certain decorations

anti-Saxonism: avoidance of words from the Anglo-Saxon

antibeheadment: beheadment that generates contrasting word: bonus, lawful, preview, shell

anticdotal: [antic + anecdotal portmanteau] referring to retelling of humorous experience

anticharade: charade that is its own antonym: no where ≠ now here, un-huhn ≠ unh-unh

anticipatory plagiarism:

antidiluvian: [antediluvian mondegreen] disbeliever in the Biblical flood

antigram: anagram with opposite meaning of original word: adversaries = are advisers, astronomers = no more stars, diplomacy = mad policy, enormity = more tiny, evangelists = evil's agents, filled = ill-fed, forget-me-not = forgotten me, funeral = real fun, giant = I, gnat, infection = fine tonic, lemonade = demon ale, militarism = I limit arms, misfortune = it's more fun, protectionism = nice to imports, united = untied, violence = nice love

antimetabole: repeating words in opposite order

antipophora: self-answering

antirebus: words read as letters: "Oh, Any" (one), "I see why." (icy)

antiroo: aka antikangaroo, describes word with antonym within: communicative (mute), friend (fiend), pest (pet), wnderful (woeful)

antu: [abusus non tollit usum acronym] inexcusable abuse

anvilope: [anvil + envelope portmanteau] paper covering for blacksmith tool

Anx: [beheaded Manx] poem with initial and terminal lines, word with initial or terminal letters, or number with initial and terminal digits deleted

anymal: [animal + -nym portmanteau] describes animal name that is used as a verb: ape, badger, bat, bird-dog, bug, carp, crab, crane, crow, dog, fawn, flounder, fly, goose, grub, kid, leech, parrot, perch, slug, sponge, tick, weasel, wolf, worm

aoad: [Aesop acronym] "Appearances often are deceiving."

aolawo: [Napoleon acronym] "Ability's of little account without opportunity."

apae: ["a posse ad esse", (from possibility to actuality) acronym] actualization

aparently: [apparent mondegreen] acting as mother and/or father

apethy: [ape + apathy portmanteau] state at which primates become used to Humans

apfyt: [Lyly acronym] "A penny for your thought."

aphaeresis: omission of initial syllable or letter: 'pataphysics

apimawth: [Phillips Brooks acronym] "A prayer ... is merely a wish turned heavenward."

Apocalyptic: power of two with six hundred sixty-six digits, or two-to-the-two-thousand-tenth, $2^{2,010}$ -eleventh, $2^{2,011}$, or -twelfth, $2^{2,012}$

apocope: deleting part of a word: cinema, curio, taxi, th'

apophasis: insinuation that denies what's said: *Julius Caesar* 3:2:79ff

aposiopesis: not completing thought

apostronym: [Dave Morice's apostrophe word] word that becomes another word with apostrophe deletion: can't, he'll, I'll, she'll, we'd, we'll, we're

apostrophy: [apostrophe mondegreen] award given for good punctuation

appmae: ["Adde parvum parvo magnus acervus erit". acronym] add little by little and there will be a big pile

apropoe: [apropos + Poe portmanteau] fitting for a work of Edgar Allen Poe

apsiape: [acronym] "A penny save is a penny earned."

aptogram: [apt anagram for given word] star pine = pinaster, Florence Nightingale = flit on, cheering angel, Quid est veritas? = Est vir adest. Albert Einstein = bent lines are it, telegraph = great help, punishment = nine thumps, received payment = every cent owed me, train = it ran, French Revolution = violence run forth, Washington crossing the Delaware = he saw his ragged Continentals row, astronomers = moonstarers, Adolph Hitler = hated for ill, Henry Wadsworth Longfellow = won half the New World's glory, Robert Louis Stevenson = our best novelist, se¤or, Dante Gabriel Rossetti = greatest idealist born, Oliver Wendell Holmes = he'll do in a mellow verse

aptronym: self-describing name: Dan Druff, Honor Foote, Moses Grass, Rex Holmes, Sally Ride

aqa: [Age quod agis. acronym] do what you do (well), pay attention to what you are doing.

aquadextrous: with ability to turn the bathtub faucet on and off with your toes

aqualibrium: [aqua + equilibrium portmanteau] point where the stream of a drinking fountain water is at a Goldilock height

Arabian: [*1,001 Arabian Nights*] with one thousand one digits, $1001 \leq \log n < 1002$

arbinger: [harbinger + arbor portmanteau] lone tree which indicates a nearby grove, wood or forest

arkade: [ark -ade compound] what Noah's family drank on shipboard

ard: [beheaded ord with phonetic r-] word that has been doubly beheaded

Ardunian: [beheaded Erdunian with phonetic r-] with first two and last four lines unwritten

area: product of a number's height in stacked tens or tetrarithm, and its length in digits or rounded logarithm

arithmetization: transformation as in Gödel coding of wffs into integers

arithmogram: aka number name anagram, word whose letters can be rearranged into a number name: eon (one), ether (three), net (ten), there (three), tow (two)

arithmonymous: describes a word which contains the letters of at least one number name: interchangeability (three, eight, nine, ten, thirteen, thirty, thirty-nine, eighty, eighty-nine, ninety, ninety-eight)

arithmopoem: number in the form of a poem, like Abraham Lincoln's couplet "four score"

arrational: [beheaded irrational with phonetic r-] between rational and irrational

artailment: [beheaded curtailment beheadment with phonetic r-] simultaneous double beheading and curtailment, $[(n - 10^{logn}[n/10^{logn\,-1}])/10]$

armups: [up in arms wordle] aroused to action

arrational: [beheaded irrational with phonetic r-] between rational and irrational

arty choke: [artichoke mondegreen] gag reflect triggered by bad artwork

asankheya: [Sanskrit] ten-to-the-hundred-fortieth, fortyplex, 10^{140}

ascenderless: letter without ascender: a, c, e, g, i, j, m, n, o, p, q, r, s, u, v, w, x, y, z

aseunggi: [Sino-Korean] ten-to-the-fifty-sixth, fifty-sixplex, 10^{56}

ask aunt: [askance mondegreen] seek advice from mother's sister

asshas: [acronym] "A sorrow shared's half a sorrow."

assonance: with vowel sound only rhymed

assymetrical: describing letters (F, G, J, L, N, P, Q, R, S, Z) or digits (2, 3, 4, 5, 6, 7, 9) that are not symmetrical

aster-risk: [asteroid risk portmanteau, asterisk hyphenym] odds of being hit by a falling star

astrocomical: [astronomical + comical portmanteau] describes when astronomer's pronouncements are humorous: "We never expected that! "

astroillogical: [astrological + illogical portmanteau] demonstrating the logically extrapolated illogicalness of astrology

astronomical: [Scott Aaronson] on the order of $99^{99} \approx 10^{200}$

astronumby: [numb + astronomy portmanteau] mind-numbing, gee-whiz astronomy

asyndeton: with conjunctions, articles, or even pronouns deleted

atata: [Sanskrit] ten-to-the-eighty-fourth, eight-fourplex, 10^{84}

atging: [Cervantes acronym] "All that glitters is not gold."

atofl: [Manilius acronym] "All things obey fixed laws."

atponhsip: [Emerson acronym] "Adopt the pace of Nature; her secret is patience."

attentative: [tentative + attentive portmanteau] paying attention, but not very much

attractive: describes homonymous antonyms: daughter (mother), evening (morning), left (right), man (woman),

audiomancy: [audio- -mancy compound] act of trying to identify a gift by holding it to your ear and shaking it

auktioneer: [auk + auctioneer portmanteau] someone who tries to sell seabirds

auntagonist: [antagonist mondegreen] someone contributing to their mother's sister's agony, bad uncle

auntylope: [antelope mondegreen] run off to marry your mother's sister

audioactive: number string that transmutes into another under look-and-say operation, unium, protocalcium, uranium, biunium, triunium, tribium, protobitrium, unbitrium, biuntrium, bitriunium, promethium, tribiunium, zinc, but not hydrogen

auliaed: [Goehe acronym] "A useless life is an easy death."

auntonym: [aunt + antonym portmanteau] aka cleonym, name of one's parent's sister, especially if Cleo

auto-biography: [autobiography hyphenym] car's history

autological: [Grelling's paradox] word that describes itself: autological, finished, visible

autophone: [automobile sound] one of the seven car noises or 42 combinations

	grind	hiss	knock	rattle	scrape	squeak	thump

grind		griss	grock	grattle	grape	greak	grump
hiss	hind		hock	hattle	hape	heak	hump
knock	knind	kniss		knattle	knape	kneak	knump
rattle	rind	riss	rock		rape	reak	rump
scrape	scrind	scriss	scrock	scrattle		screak	scrump
squeak	squind	squiss	squock	squattle	squape		squump
thump	thrind	thiss	thock	thattle	thrape	theak	

autantonym: word that is its own antonym: annul, bested, bone, cavalier, cleave, counterpart, dress, dust, fast, husk, let, loose, mortal, nervous, overlook, ravel, seeded, shell, temper, think better, trim, trip, unbending, weather, wind

automynoragram: [Howard Bergerson] self-referential acronymous passage: "Exquisite, Xavier! Quite unparalleled, I'd say, in textured esprit..."

autoshiftgram: word which is its own shiftgram, tanger + 13 = gnatre, emblazonry + 13 = rzoynmbael

avalanche: word rhope

ava: [ad vitam aeternam acronym] for eternity

avav: [a verbis ad verbera acronym] from words to blows

avera: [amicus verus est rara avis acronym] a true friend is rare

avo: [amor vincit omnia acronym] love conquers all

avoidabull: [avoidable mondegreen] what bullfighters do

awall: [AWOL mondegreen] escape by climbing over barrier

awfulmologist: [awful + optholmogist portmanteau] very bad eye doctor

awtew: [Shakespeare acronym] "All's well that ends well."

awkword: pronounceable non-word as in conlangs (constructed languages) with consonant, vowel selections and patterns

ayuta: [Sanskrit] ten-to-the-nineth, nineplex, 10^9

azzification: [beheaded zazzification] insertion of -az- to turn a non-slang word into slang or make a word slangier, as in billion to bazillion

b-devoiced: describes word whose b is changed to d: bane (Dane), bank (dank), bare (dare), bay (day),

b-est: [extrapolated from Aronson numbers] number described in Latin statement, "B est prima littera in hic sententiam, non seconda, ..."

b-invariant: describing word with b in 2nd place: ab, abaci, abacus, aback, abft, abase, abate, abbess, abbey, abbot, abduct, abeam, abet, abhor, abide, abject, adjure, able, abler, ...

babetnaa: [Camden acronym] "Better a bad excuse than none at all."

back-formation: [James Murray] forming another word by removing or replacing affix, ante-, anti-, co-, con-, de-, dis-, en-, -er, -est, ex-, fore-, il-, im-, in-, -ing, ir-, pre-, pro-, post-, pre-, re-, sub-, super-, un-, uni-

background: probability of positive test, which increases false-positives

backlash: [back + lash portmanteau] lash that grows backward like ingrown hair or naie

backswitch: changing the tail digit or letter and reversing the rest of the number or word

bacronym: [David Parlett] half of a semordnilap, a word which when spelled backward gives another word, like palindromes and semordnilap, buns, door, desserts, diaper, doom, dray,

edit, emit, evil, gnat, keel, leek, liar, live, loop, mar, mart, mood, nap, naps, net, new, nip, nips, not, nuts, pan, pans, pets, pin, pool, pools, pot, pots, rail, ram, rats, rebut, redraw, repaid, rood, sloop, smart, snap, snaps, snub, snoops, span, spin, spoons, spots, star, step, stop, stops, stressed, stun, tang, ten, tide, time, ton, top, tram, trams, tuber, warder, wen, yard
backword: pure word with letters from the back half of the alphabet, n-to-z: nonsupports
bae: ["before all else" acronym] most highly valued
baek: [Sino-Korean] hundred, twoplex, 10^2
bagair: [airbag back-formation] explosive layer of air atop a potato chip bag
Bagari: describes words which change to another word when a double vowel with a b between is reduced to the vowel: abaft (aft), awash (ash), flyby (fly), hobo (ho), ibid (id), ibis (is), robot (rot), see Af Jinni
bahttaet: [Thomas Fuller paraphrase acronym] "Better a hen tomorrow than an egg today."
bahula: [Sanskrit] ten-to-the-twenty-third, twenty-threeplex, 10^{23}
baked bads: [baked goods antonym] what the baker rejects as failed efforts
Baker's glerint: [Anglo-Ferengi] thirteen-to-the-sixth, $13^6 = 4,826,809$
Baker's gross: [dozen:gross:Baker's dozen:?] thirteen cubed, $13^3 = 2,197$
balanced: middleweight number with average digit weight of exactly 4.5, like 90; word with wordnum = 13.: by, lo, wizard, acronyms, flourish, jealousy, kinology, literary, logology, lyricism, snowlike, souplike, twilight, valorize, blizzardly, immodestly, immorality, immunizing, multiplier, abstruseness, razzle-dazzle, intermenstral, progenitorship, transitionally, uncrystallized, quantitativeness
balder dash: [balderdash mondegreen] fast-moving receding hairline
baldface: [boldface mondegreen] shameless as a crash test dummy
Baldy's Law: "Some of anything plus the rest of anything equals the whole thing."
ballad: 4343-syllabled quatrain rhymed abcb
balweighedance: [weighed in the balance wordle] found wanting
bamnesia: [bam + amnesia portmateau] losing one's memory after getting hit on the head
Banach-Tarski paradox: a ball cab be cut into a finite number of pieces and re-assemble to get two balls, each of equal size to the first.
banangram: [Harry Matthews' ban + anagram portmanteau] meaningless anagram
band-done: [abandon mondegreen] break taken along with the band when they stop playing
bang: [computerese] exclamation mark, symbol for factorial, n!
banjax: [paleologism] break
bannedwagon: [bandwagon mondegreen] kind of wagon forbidden within certain locations by law
baraka: [Arabic] spiritual energy or aura of blessedness created when a person or group touches Oneness that empowers that person, group or even places or objects
barbarian: [from -barbar] ten-to-the-three-thousandth higher, $10^{3,000}n$
barbarianism: [Chris McManus] binade with a strike-out: barbarianism (brains), beauty (bat), ristle (bite), buoyant (boat), bureau (bra), feast (fat), presto (pet)
barbecutie: [barbecue + cutie portmanteau] good-looking barbecuer
barbee: [barber back-formation] person who has had a shave and/or a haircut
barbequeue: [barbecue + queue portmanteau] line that form waiting for BBQ
barbitrator: [barbecue + arbitrator portmanteau] person who makes peace in a barbequeue
bardo: [Tibetan] mental state transitional between fear and longing, sanity and insanity, confusion and wisdom, life and Life

Barnum's Law: [P. T. Barnum] You'll never go broke underestimating the intelligence of the American public.

barren waist: [barren waste mondegreen] naked midriff

barrendipity: [barren + serendipity portmanteau] not finding what you're seeking where you expect to find it

baseggsket: [eggs in one basket wordle] over-dependence

buttered cat paradox: Although cats land on their feet, toast usually lands butter-side down.

bauftaum: [James Ellis acronym] "Better an ugly face than an ugly mind."

bawdrize: [bawdry + -ze] unbowdlerize, make word more offensive, like "family" to "famdamnily"

bebious: ["believe everyone believes it." acronym back-formation] believing that all others believe

bebushat: [beat around the bush wordle] delay

Becker's Law: Finding a job's more difficult than keeping one.

bedlock: [bed + wedlock portmanteau] bondage to one's co-fornicator before marriage

bedspread: mondegreen] feast-in-bed

beek: [Scotch, beak homonym] warm, bask

beer: [Restaurantese rootbeer squared] fifty-five squared, $55^2 = 3,025$

beergardener: [beer garden back-formation] frequenter of an outdoor beer-drinking establishment

beforelife: [afterlife back-formation] this life before the life after this

beggeer: [egg in beer wordle] out-of-place object

belike: [paleologism] most likely, probably

belle absente: acrostic in which a name is encoded lipogrammatically

beluthahatchee: [Afro-American] legendary, blissful, dreamy state where all wrongs are forgiven and forgotten

belbatsfry: [bats in belfry wordle] insanity

bellibone: [paleologism] woman excelling both in beauty and goodness, fair maiden

belliclose: [bellicose + close portmanteau] eager for hand-to-hand combat

Benchley's Law: "Anyone can do any amount of work, provided it isn't the work he is supposed to be doing at that moment."

Benford's law: In any collection of statistics, a given statistic has roughly a 30% chance of starting with the digit 1.

bergette: rondeau with 1 strophe and refrain deleted

Berkeley's Laws: (1) "Most problems have either many answers or no answer, few a single answer." (2) "An answer may be wrong, right, both, or neither; most are both." (3) "A chain of reasoning is no stronger than its weakest link." (4) "An exception tests a rule; it never proves it." (5) "If there is an opportunity to make a mistake, sooner or later it will be made." (6) "Being sure mistakes will occur is a good frame of mind for catching them." (7) "A great many problems do not have accurate answers, but do have approximate ones, from which sensible decisions can be made."

Berra's Law: [Yogi Berra] You can observe a lot just by watching.

betical: [alphabetical contraction] with consonants in alphabetical order, see alphal

be-wilder: [bewilder hyphenym] make less controllable

bhoc: [John Heywood acronym] "By hook or crook"

bi-inary: refering to number system based on 2i

bi-nib: [mynynym] pen with two nibs

bi-sacksual: [bisexual + sack portmanteau] able to accept either paper or plastic sack for groceries

bialphabetical: describes word able to be separated into just two alphabetical sequences: femininity = fmnnty + eiii, see rollercoaster

bibious: ["B(elieve) I b(elieve) i(t.)" acronym back-formation] believing that another should believe that you believe

bicephalous: describes word able to be behead and still be a word: bright, cat, chaste, cowl, denunciate, eat, elector, emotion, ere, fright, gastronomical, ion, junction, knight, man, methyl, ore, never, pathetic, praise, race, revolve, ram, rash, rend, slander, tern, tray, treason, your, zone

bicycle: two-word compound or phrase that can be swapped into another compound or phrase: boathouse ≠ house boat

bicyclopedia: [bicycle + encyclopedia portmanteau] cycling guidebook

bicicle: [bi- + icicle portmanteau] icicle with two points

bidbious: ["B(elieve) I d(on't) b(elieve) i(t)." anagram back-formation] believing that another should believe that you do not believe

bidious: ["B(elieve) I d(isbelieve) i(t.)" acronym back-formation] believing that another should believe that you disbelieve

bifurgation: fallacy of limiting argument to just two positions: "Have you stopped beating your wife?"

big-headed: [bigheaded hyphenym] describing a word beginning with big- but not referring to big: bigamy, bigot, bigamist, bigotry

biga peula: [New Guinean Kiriwina] expressing inexpressible mokitas

big-a-mist: [bigamist hyphenym] large Italian fogbank

biheadment: [bigram + beheadment portmanteau] deleting the first two letters of a word: alone (one), aspirate (pirate), liberating (berating), start (art), there (ere), see back-formation

bimot: [François Le Lionnais] product of former (articles, possessives, auxiliaries) and signifier (substantives, transitives) matrices giving all combinations

binade: alternade able to be broken by alternating letters into two smaller words: calliopes = clips + aloe, triennially = tinily + renal

Binary Law: "There are 10 kinds of people in the world, those who think in binary and those who don't."

bindu: [Sanskrit] ten-to-the-forty-ninth, forty-nineplex, 10^{49}

binns: [paleologism] glasses

bious: ["Believe it!" anagram back-formation] believing that another should believe

birr: [bird back-formation] what a bird has done to it, stalked by predators

bisograms: pair of isograms: blacksmith, gunpowder

bitoth: [Carlyle acronym] "Biography is the only true history."

bitsol: [Swift acronym] "Bread is the staff of life."

bitsow: [Shakespeare acronym] "Brevity is the soul of wit."

bivwhack: [bivouac mondegreen] surprize attack at temporary encampment

Blauw's Law: Established technology tends to persist in spite of new technology.

blench: [paleologism] shrink, flinch, quail

blackholing: transformation of number into another, such as by HOTPO (half-or-triple-plus-one), DENEAT (digits-even-not-even-and total) operations

blessed: describes word beginning with bl- that generates a fictitious name, Bl. Ack, Bl. Ah, Bl. Ameless, Bl. Astoff, Bl. Azing, Bl. Esser, Bl. Ind, Bl. Iss, Bl. Oody, Bl. Uenose

blik: unalterable belief that transcends the mere facts made possible by them, like paranoids' "They're after me!" or uniformitarians' "The future will be like the past."

blind: refers to number without an i in its name, like zero, one, two, three, four

blorunsod: [runs in the blood] genetically inherited

blowwhole: [blowhole + whole portmanteau] spend a whale of a lot on something almost nothing

blueoncemoon: [once in a bluemoon wordle] rarely

blue-seven phenomenon: blue and seven are most commonly picked color and number (next to red and three)

blunder-bus: [blunderbus hyphenym] bus that could easily be involved in an accident

bo: [million : mo :: billion : ?] two-greats gross, twelve-to-the-fourth, $12^4 = 20,736$

boafft: [acronym] "Birds of a feather flock together."

bofeelnes: [feel in bones wordle] feel deeply

Bohr's Law: The crazier the theory, the more likely it's correct, the harder it is to understand, and the more likely it is to be published.

Bok's Law: "The cost of education is nothing compared to the cost of ignorance."

bowler-skater: [bowler + iceskater portmanteau] participant in the short-lived sport of bowling-on-ice

bomb-enable: [abominable mondegreen] start the countdown for a timed explosion

bonnbet: [b(ee) in bonnet wordle] angry

Boob's Law: You will always find what you're looking for in the last place you look.

book-keeper: [bookkeeper hyphenym] person who won't return a borrowed book

bookend: word or number divisible into a word or number formed from its ends and its middle: betrayer = beer + tray, debater = deer + bat, ligament = lint + game, money = my one, resident = rent + side

Booker's Law: An ounce of application is worth a ton of abstraction. (16000:1)

boolean: [*Poémes booléens* by François Le Lionnais] intersection or symmetric differences of two works: of two novels as done by J. Duchateau

Borkowski's Law: You can't guard against the arbitrary.

borderstate: [stately extrapolation] describes stately words ending in a state abbreviation: almond, avail, dolphin, jackal, mayor, sunny

bosbandton: [banned in Boston wordle] obscene by local standards

botif: [Aesop acronym] "Beware of the insincere friend."

bottomsy-turvy: [back-formation] topsy-turvy antonym, normal-side-down

boundless: [mondegreen] unable to leap or jump

boustrophedon: [Grk. "as the ox turns"] alternatingly left-to-right and right-to-left: "Mary had a little Lamb. wons sa etihw saw eseelf s'tl"

boustrophedonym: word divisible into two letter strings one alphabetical, one zyxical

boustrophedonum: [boustrophedon number palindrome] number divisible into alternating increscendo and decrescendo frags, like 1012 or 1210 into 12 and 10

bouts-rimés: [Dulot, Fren. "rhymed ends"] verse composed from given rhymes

bowl-egged: [bowlegged hyphenym] having eggs in the egg bowl

bowlling: [bowling mondegreen] small bowl

boxtopography: [boxtop + topography portmanteau] art and science of box top collecting

boy ant: [boyant mondegreen] young male ant said to float

boycot: [boycott mondegreen] young man's simple bed

Boyle's Laws: (1) The deficiency will never show itself during the dry runs. (2) Clearly stated instructions will consistently produce multiple interpretations.
boys-in-berries: [boysenberries mondegreen] young men in a berry patch
boysterous: [boisterous mondegreen] as noisy as a mollusk, that is, very quiet
bozone: [bozo zone portmanteau] area of contamination within earshot of foolish people making others foolish, at least by association
brachylogia: abridged expression: "And he to England shall along with you." (*Hamlet* III, iii by William Shakespeare)
bradoubless: [double in brass wordle] moonlight
braggadossier: [braggadocio + dossier portmanteau] collection of personal information that makes the person look too good to be true
Brahinsky's number: eight-to-the-ninth factorial, $8^9! = 134,217,728!$
braintryst: [brain tryst portmanteau ≈ braintrust] meeting of minds
braised: [John Berryman's berrichonne] describes poem with lines using consonance and assonance and rhyme
bran-dish: [brandish hyphenym] recipe using outer layers of grain
brattled: [brat + rattled portmanteau] uncomfortable feeling that laughing children are laughing at you, when they're probably not, like those in a school bus
breakfast: [breakfast homonym] stop suddenly when the traffic light changes
breaking news: reports of latest new record during the Olympics
breatharian: [vegetarian : vegan :: vegan : ?] person who feeds on just air
brewhaha: [brouhaha mondegreen] jolly tea party
bricker: [paleologism] shoplift, steal
bricoleur: [French] tinkerer who constructively messes around without a preconceived plan
briefly: writing and talking faster to fill all available time
Brooke's Law: "Whenever a system becomes completely defined, some fool discovers something which either abolishes the system or expands it beyond recognition."
brool: [paleologism] low roar, deep murmur or humming
bubble-gum: unrealistic, but with engaging characters and exciting plot, focusing on language, like *The Fan Man* by William Kotzwinkle
bubious: ["B(elieve yo)u b(elieve) i(t.)" grammanym back-formation] believing that another should believe that they believe
buckdropet: [drop in bucket wordle] something seemingly negligible
Bucy's Law: Nothing worthwhile has ever been accomplished by a reasonable man.
budbious: ["B(elieving yo)u d(on't) b(elieve) i(t.)" grammanym back-formation] believing that another should believe that they do not believe
bulgasaui: [Sino-Korean] ten-to-the-sixty-fourth, sixty-fourplex, 10^{64}
bull: [Obadiah Bull] almost reasonable juxtaposition of incongruities: "Half the lies he tells are not true!", "I boldly answer in the affirmative: No!", "I would not have sold my only pot but I needed to buy something to put in it.", "I hope that I may live to hear you preach my funeral.", "I marvel at the strength of human weakness!", "If I have any prejudice against him, it is in his favor.", "If you don't like it, sit down and get out!", "If you have not received this message, please write me and let me know.", "We are not responsible for acts of God, Indians or other public enemies of the government.", Of All Things Knowable and More, "This report is full of omissions!"
bull-headed: [bullheaded mondegreen] describing a word beginning with bull- but not referring to bulls: bulla, bullet, bulletin, bullion

Bunuel's Law: Overdoing things is harmful in all cases, even when it comes to efficiency.
buried: describes word within a word, either contiguous or discontiguous: meat = at, eat, et, mat, me, met
busillis: baffling puzzle or difficult point
butt-in-law: [butt-in + in-law portmanteau] spouse's meddlesome family
butt-tress: [buttress mondegreen] long braid reaching to a woman's rear end
buylateral: [buy + bilateral portmanteau] purchase "on the side" though not actually "under the table"
buzz: multiple of five, 5n
byr a thoddaid: [Welsh] couplet with 8-syllable verses plus 10- and 6-syllable verses with a before-end rhyme in 3rd verse and alliterative or assonance after or rhymed last verse
c-chest: [sea chest mondegreen] chest (chess on a triangular board) spelled with a C, not spelled palindromically tshehst
C-graphable: [cannonball or tetrahedon, Leonard Gordon] word graphable as if in 3-D tetrahedral tiling: supercalifragilistic-expialidocious
c-invariant: word with c in 3rd place: arc, arch, arcs, back, buck, cock, deck, deco, dice, doc, dock, duck, duct, each, etch, face, fact, foci, focus, hack, hic, hick, hock, inca, inch, ...
cab age: [cabbage mondegreen] how old a taxi is
cabinette: [cabinet mondegreen] small cabin
cablemite: hypothetical insect pest related to
cadence: describes letters or digits equally spaced within a word or number: effervencence, noncontamination
cafeatherp: [feather in cap wordle] something to be proud of
Cagari: describes words which change to another word when a double vowel with a c between is reduced to the vowel: caucuses (causes), dicing (ding), loco (lo), priciest (priest), teacake (teak), see Af Jinni
cahoot: [sing. cahoots] would-be conspirator
cahul: ["Cave ab homine unius libri." acronym] Beware of anyone who has just one book.
calculust: [calculation lust portmanteau ≈ calculus] mathematical obsessive-compulsion
Calembaurnus: [James Joyce, from calembour] patron saint of pun
calenture: [paleologism] fever formerly supposed to affect sailors in the tropics
calaesthentics: [calisthenics + aesthetics portmanteau] Olympic-class beautiful gymnastics
callousthenics: [callous + calisthenics portmanteau] strenuous exercises that may leave callouses
camarowderie: [camaraderie + rowdy portmanteau] noisy partying among friends
camel lot: [Camelot mondegreen] parking space for desert nomads
cancrine: word numberdrome, such as one hundred one
candlelite: [candlelight mondegreen] small candle for children
candonym: [can do word] n-letter word like can which can be transformed into another word by adding pairs of letters' values (3, 1, 14) to get those for an (n - 1)-letter word, like do (4, 15)
cantainer: [can + container portmanteau] paper or plastic holder for multiple cans
cantibal: [cannibal antonym] person who would rather die that have to eat another person
cantankerush: [cantanterous + rush portmanteau] mad dash of crowd toward sale items
cento: aka patchwork, mosaic, work put together from many other's works
capex: [cap + apex portmanteau] button atop a baseball cap
capitalism: textual shouting by writing in CAPITOLS

capitonym: word that changes pronunciation and meaning when not capitalized: August, Fall, May, Nice, Polish, Spring, Tangier

capped: [capt- mondegreen] describes word beginning with capt- that generates a fictitious name: Capt. Ivator, Capt. Tan, Capt. Tor

capsize: mondegreen] turn over, such as a hat, to determine how big it is

capstand: [capstan mondegreen] hatrack for caps

car tune: [cartoon mondegreen] song heard or sung while in an automobile

cardevilnate: [devil incarnate wordle] very evil person

carpool: variation on bumper cars with side pockets

carded: describes word with playing card symbol letters (A, J, K, Q): q̲ua̲cks̲alver

cart blank: [carte blanche mondegreen] with an empty cart

casbairdne: [Irish] 7-syllabled stanza of quatrain rhymed abcb with a and c consonate and at least 2 verses with 2 crossrhymes

cashtration: [cash + castration portmanteau] act of buying a house which renders the buyer financially impotent for an indefinite period

catachresis: incorrect word choice, see malapropism

caterpallor: [caterpillar + pallor portmanteau] loss of skin color when finding a worm in one's food

caudation: operation of adding a new final letter or digit, as in multiplying a non-multiple of ten by ten or adding a non-zero digit to a multiple of ten

cayaoh: [1 Pet 5:7 acronym] "Cast all your anxiety on Him."

Cayo's Law: The only time an event will start on time's when you're not.

caw ithhoots: [in cahoots with wordle] co-conspirator of

cehe: ["Cur etiam hic es?" acronym] Why are you still here?

celebation: [celebacy + celebration portmanteau] feast in honor of priestly vocation

cello mold: [jello mold mondegreen] mold that tends to grow on a little-used cello

cellular: [Conway's game of life] "life" and "death" of elements defined by initial organization (alphabetical, lexical, syntactic, semantic, ...) and metabolic changes

cento: aka mosaic, text composed from passages from other texts

central: number whose number name is central when an odd number of number names is alphabetized

centrifugal: not too fugal or too unfrugal

cev: ["Credere est videre." acronym] Believing is seeing

chain: words linked by a shared characteristic, see anagrammar, homoliteral, homo nimble

chain-link sentence: homoliteral in which words share initial bigram (for example) with predecessor's final and final bigram with successor's initial: "Frankenstein intimidated Edith through ghoulish shenanigans.", "The helium umbrella lacked edging.", "Wine never erases essential aloneness."

chain conundrum: conundrum with homonimble solution, in the form: "Why is a ... like a ...?"

chairful: [cheerful + chair portmanteau] with just enough chairs before the music stops and there is suddenly one two few

chalkolate: [chalk + chocolate portmanteau] brown-colored sidewalk chalk

chandlerism: [Raymond Chandler] risk, metaphor in the form "She was the kind of woman who could make a grocer grosser.", "... a bricklayer laybricks."

changeover: change of a word into another by changing and moving over one letter: h̲olster = oldst̲er

chank: [paleologism] chew noisily

chant royal: 5(11) + 5 = 60-syllable poem rhyming ababccddedE plus ddedE envoi

charade: aka redivider, string able to be punctuated in more than one way: "Flamingo, pale, scenting a latent shark!" ≈ "Flaming, opalescent in gala tents: hark!", "O, had a man developed a way!" ≈ "Oh, Adam and Eve loped away.", see hyphenym

charadrome: [charade + palindrome portmanteau] word divided into smaller words that can be read backward and reassembled as another word: supermathematical = sup + er + mat + he + ma + tic + al = la + cit + am + eh + tam + re + pus = lacitamehtamrepus

charitable: [David Silverman] word which remains a word with any single-letter deletion or number that retains property with any single-digit deletion: pleats = leats, peats, plats, plets, pleas, pleat

charlaquin: [charlatan + harlequin portmanteau] clown that's not at all funny, killer klown

charp: [paleologism] bed, sleep

chattle: [chat + chattel portmanteau] one's whole vocabulary even the small talk, not just the big impressive words

cheap: with one, two or three

cheaper: with one and two or two and three or one and three

cheapest: with one, two and three

checkout: [mondegreen] examining someone you don't immediately recognize until who they are registers

chee: ["Cujusvis hominis est errare."acronym] to err is Human

chekkuautodibaida: [Jap.] bar at a checkout line that separates one customer's groceries from another's

chessque: [chess + -esque poertmanteau] describing word with chess symbol letters (B, K, N, P, Q, R): bankrupt, barbarian, knapsack, quicksand

chesspeace: [chess piece mondegreen] end of a friendly chess game that ends without a dispute

chesspool: [chess + pool portmanteau, ≈ cesspool] "on-deck" lesser chessplayers waiting to play the master chessplayer

chetongueek: [tongue in cheek wordle] not seriously

chiaroscuro: joy and sorrow, hope and dispair, …

chiclé: Spoonerized cliché: tacitest (from acid test)

chimera: work with the nouns, verbs, adjectives replaced from three other works

chinabullshop: [bull in china shop wordle] very accidentally destructive

Chisholm's Second Law: When things are going well, something will go wrong.

Chiteana: [tea in China wordle] something very valuable

choka: 5,7-syllabled verses ending with 77

choirantine: [choir + quarantine portmanteau] sequester singers until the performance

chompanzee: [chomp + chimpanzee portmanteau] noisy eater

choop: [paleologism] scram

chorecast: [chore + forecast portmanteau] particularly bad weather forecast that implies shoveling or scraping ice from a windshield

choreography: [chore + choreography portmanteau] art of charting who does which household chores when

chronogram: [*Art of Chronogram*, Brussels, 1718, etc.] Roman numerals in text indicate date, even if anagrammic and irregular, even acronymic: chronogram = 900, "Christvs Dux ero trivmphvs" = MDCXVVVII = 1627, mix = 1009, "Videbvnt in qvem transfixervnt." (Jn 19:37)

= MDXVVVVIII =1533 [Michael Stifelius], "My [Queen Elizabeth I] day closed is in immortality."
= 1603
chou: [Jap.] ten-to-the-twelfth, twelveplex, 10^{12}
chumpire: [chum + chump + umpire portmanteau] umpire that can be considered friendly or unfriendly depending upon which side he decides in favor of or against
cielito: [Span. "little heaven"] 8-syllable quatrain rhymed abcb
cinquain: 5-verse stanza
cieopoeic: [-poeic mynynym] having to do with creating palindromes or numberdromes
circularity: continuing the same operation over and over: "I made a mistake ..."
circtalkles: [talk in circles wordle] obfuscate
circulate: exponentially stack to infinity, $n\uparrow^\infty n' = n\rightarrow n'\rightarrow\infty = g(\infty, n', n)$
ciscendentals: [trans- : cis- :: transcendental : ?] surreal numbers derived by enversion from reals, below transcendentals
citoi: [see eye to eye wordle] mutually agree
Citpylacopa: [Apocalyptic ananym] reverse Apocalyptic
clang: apparently unrelated word association resulting from turning a word backward and/or fragmenting it: golf with flog or log
claptomaniac: [cleptomaniac + clap portmanteau] applause stealer, ham
Clarke's Laws: [Arthur C. Clarke] (1) When a distinguished but elderly scientist states that something is possible, he is almost certainly right; when he states that something is impossible, he is very probably wrong. (2) The only way to discover the limits of the possible is to go beyond them into the impossible. (3) Any sufficiently advanced technology is indistinguishable from magic.
clearly: ignoring the intermediate steps
cleek: [paleologism] wet blanket
clerihaiku: [clerihu, haiku portmanteau] mnemonic 3-line poem with proper name as first line with 5 + 7 + 5 = 17 syllables
clerihew: [Edmund Clerihew Bentley] mnemonic 4-verse poem with proper name as first verse rhyming aabb, "The digestion of Milton Was unequal to Stilton. He was only feeling so-so When he wrote 'Il Penseroso'.","George the Third Ought never to have occured. One can only wonder At so gross a blunder.", "Sir Christopher Wren Said, "I'm going to dine with some men. If anybody calls, Say I'm designing St. Paul's.", "Sir Humphrey Davy Abominated gravy. He lived in the odium Of having discovered sodium.", "Sir James Jeans Always says what he means. He is really perfectly serious About the universe being mysterious."
clime: [climb + climate portmanteau] move to a higher altitude for cooler temperatures
clinamen: [swerving] assymetry, anti-constraint or imbalance in a system that proves free will over determinism
clipt: [clipped contraction] shorter respelling of word
clogyrnach: [Welsh] 8 + 2 + 5 + 3 + 3 + 2 = 23-syllabled poem rhyming aabbba
cloheaduds: [head in clouds wordle] out-of-touch with reality
clolivever: [live in clover wordle] live happily ever after
Clopton's Law: For every credibility gap there's an overabundance of gullibility.
clothes-spins: [clothes spin hyphenym] what spin cycle of washing machine does, replaced clothes pins
closkeletonset: [skeleton in closet wordle] still hidden scandal
Clyde's Law: The longer you put off something that needs doing, the greater the probability that it'll be done by someone else.

cnalurt: [Isa 1:18 acronym] "Come now and let us reason together."

coao: ["claude os, aperi oculos" acronym] shut mouth, open eyes

coddepencency: [codependency mondegreen] fear of losing one's codpiece

co-dean: [codeine mondegreen] one who shares the office of dean at a college or university

codswallop: [paleologism] nonsense

Cohn's Law: The more time you spend in reporting on what you are doing, the less time you have to do anything.

coin-cidence: [coincidence hyphenym] unusual event involving coins

collinear: describes shiftgram with proportional shifts: aped + 5 = fuji + 10 = pets, God + 8 = owl + 4 = sap + 4 = wet, gyp +1-4-3 = hum +3-12-9 = kid +1-4-3 = lea, log + 6 = rum + 2 = two, rib + 9 = ark + 3 = dun; or chain of such shifts: air + 12 = mud + 10 = wen, awl + 12 mix + 6 = sod, beef + 10 = loop + 4 = psst, bib + 12 = nun + 6 = tat, bog +6 = hum + 14 = via, bus + 6 = hay + 8 = pig, cot + 12 = oaf + 8 = win, dodo + 6 = juju + 6 = papa, elm + 3 = hop + 12 = tab, fad + 8 = nil + 6 = tor, fob + 3 = ire + 9 = ran, God + 8 = owl + 4 = sap + 4 = wet, law + 4 = pea + 4 = tie, log + 6 = run + 2 = two

coldwar: prolonged snowball fight

Cole's Law: [coleslaw] shredded cabbage with slaw dressing

coliseam: [coliseum + seam portmanteau] crack in ancient Roman stadium

collective: term for a number of things: alyses of analysts, baci of abaci, bhorred of directors, bomination of abominations, chattering of choughs, cheivement of acheivers, click of photographers, company of widgeons, complement of sycophants, concentration of thinkers, denda of additions, depth of adepts, descent of relatives, dole of adolescents, ecdote of humorists, elid of worms, entrance of actresses, a fraid of ghosts, gaggle of geese, ghast of horrors, hack of smokers, horde of prostitutes, host of angels or parasites, indifference of waiters, kimbo of arms, laddin of lamps, load of drunks, lumni of colleges, musement of mimes, nye of pheasants, ounce of announcements, patch of Apache, plump of wildfowl, pron of cooks, quaint of acquaintances, quaver of sopranos, quiver of cowards, rachnid of spiders, range of ovens, riot of students, roma of vittles, rousal of passions, rumble of basses, shrivel of critics, skein of geese, slew of dragons, sord of mallards, spring of teal, sylum of fugitives, thrill of fans, trip of dottrel, tourney of attorneys, unction of undertakers, valanche of snowballs, verage of extremes, wiggle of starlets, xiom of mathematics, ymore of anything, see animultitude

combination: word formed from two other overlapping words, not a portmanteau, whose non-overlapping letters also form a word: scarab = scar + Arab = scab, see padlock

combinatorics: [*Dissertatio de Arte Combinatoria* by J.-E. Erdmann] techniques for calculating and utilizing all combinations of text elements in hypertext: "The Theater Tree" by Paul Fournel, "A Story as You Like it" ("Un Conte … votre façon") and *100,000,000,000,000 Poems* by Raymond Queneau, matrical linguistic analysis, "The Relation X Takes Y for Z" ("La Relation x prend y pour z")

Comins's Law: People will accept your idea much more readily if you tell them Benjamin Franklin said it first.

comminkle: [commingle + mink portmanteau] associate with other upper class wearers of mink

common-tater: [commentator mondegreen] ordinary potato

composition fallacy: fallacy of implying that if p and q are true or p is true then q is not, CkpqApNq

con text: [context mondegreen] instant messaging from a prisoner

concatenation: linking digits together in a chain, as in hyperadding two and two to get twenty-two; continuing the end of one line of poem with the beginning of the next (even allowing hyphenation)

conjunction fallacy: fallacy of thinking multiple conditions are more probable than they are individually

consciousness levels: (0) unconscious, (1) subconscious, (2) subnormal, (3) normal, (4) supernormal, (7) psychic, (8) mediumistic, (9) empathic, (10) telepathic

concensus: [consensus mondegreen] count of convicts

co-gent: [cogent hyphenym] one of two gentlemen working together

coldspell: [mondegreen] spell as in a spelling bee without any advance preparation

collidoscope: [kaleidoscope mondegreen] viewer that warns if a collision is about to happen

conjested: [congested mondegreen] describing when several listeners try to tell the punchline at once

conjunktion: [conjunction + junk portmanteau] where all the garbage trucks meet

connoun: [pronoun antonym] substitute pronoun: he/she (ey, ha, heer, ne, s/he, they, thou, xe), his/her (eir, hez, hirs, hiser, hisher, nis, their, thons, xes), him/her (em, hem, himer, himmer, hir, nim, them, thon, xem)

Considine's Law: Whenever one word or letter can change the entire meaning of a sentence, the probability of an error will be in direct proportion to the resultant embarrassment.

consummé: [consume + sommé portmanteau] eat thick soup

consonance: with consonant(s) shared: cat, coat, coot, cot, cut, cute

consonant-heavy: catchphrase (8:3), latchstring (9:2), strengths (8:1)

consonantization: substituting J for I and V for U: diurnal = djvrnal

consonym: word with same consonant pattern as another: et<u>hn</u>ic = t<u>hen</u>ce

content: [area : volume :: volume : ?] measure of hyperspace

contraban: [contraband mondegreen] ban against another ban

contranym: word with contradictory meanings: aloha, bolt, duct, left, screen

conundrum: riddle question with tricky answer: "What's the difference between a fisherman and a sinner?" (One baits the hook; the other hates the Book.); "... a railway conductor and a teacher?" (One minds trains and the other trains minds.), "... a cat and a comma?" (One has claws at the end of its paws, the other a pause at the end of its clause.), "What begins with T, ends with T and is full of "T"? (teapot); "What's the largest ant?" (gi-ant) "Why is a mouse like hay?" (The cat'll eat one and the cattle eat the other.), "Which has more legs: a horse or no horse?"(No horse has ten legs.), "From what can you take the whole away and leave some?" (wholesome), "Why did the owl 'owl?" (Because the woodpecker would peck 'er.), "What comes twice in a moment yet only once in a million years?" (M), "Which word is always spelled wrong?" ("wrong"),"What's the difference between an egg and a keg?" (I'll never send you for a dozen eggs!), "Why did the "Why's it easier to read in the Fall?"(The leaves turn by themselves.), "At what time of day was Adam created?(Just before Eve.), "On which side of a building do the trees grow best?(Outside), "Why is a vacant room like a bridal suite? (Not a single person there), "Why is the Good Samaritan like a horse?" (They stop for woe.), "Why was the tomato red?" (He saw the salad dressing.), "Why do white sheep eat more than black sheep? (There're more of them.) "What should you keep after you give it to someone?" (your word)

cool ant: [coolant mondegreen] small insect adapted to below average temperatures

Cooper's Law: "In technical writing, a word not understood may be ignored with negligible loss of comprehension."

copathetic: [copacetic + pathetic portmanteau] perfectly, blissfully, wonderfully pitiable

copt: [Vauvenargues acronym] "Clearness ornaments profound thoughts."

cornfederate: [confederate + corn portmanteau] Southern moonshiner

cornucope: [cornucopia+ cope portmanteau] deal with an abundance, a windfall

correspondance: [correspondence + dance portmanteau] snail-mail or email that circumvents the main point of the response

cosmotology: [cosmology + cosmetology portmanteau] art of touching up astronomical photographs

cossante: [Span.] assonanced couplets separated by short unchanging verse

coughee: [coffee mondegreen, cougher back-formation] someone who has been coughed upon

counter-productive: [counterproductive hyphenym] efficiently delivering food to the food counter

countrified: [mondegreen] legally making a former state or province an independant country

coupeur ... la ligne: sentence(s) deletion

coutold: [out in cold wordle] miserable and alone

crackerjack-of-all-trades: [crackerjack + jack-of-all-trades portmanteau] superman who can do it all and still do it well

crambo: rhymed verses sharing no words

Cramer's paradox: The number of points of intersection of two higher-order curves can be greater than the number of arbitrary points needed to define one such curve.

crashing: [David Silverman] describes words (up to 26 letters) or numbers (up to 9 digits) with shared letter(s) or digit(s) in same position(s)

crasis: contraction of two letters or syllables into one

crenk: [paleologism] offend, irritate, annoy

Crep: [Percy Perc] reversed, curtailed and then reversed again

crescendough: [crescendo + dough portmanteau] when pastry reaches it greatest expansion

crewdriver: [beheaded screwdriver] captain or foreman who pushes those under him

Crewesque: [Crewe + -esque] poem variation with last 3 lines missing: There was a young lady of Crewe, Whose limericks stopped at line two. She was not done, after line one, but one more's all she could do.

crime wave: [mondegreen] movement of hand to signal a criminal accomplice, see hood wick

crizzle: [paleologism] roughen or crumple a surface; roughened or crumpled surface

croaker: Tom Swiftie-like sentence ending in verb rather than adverb: "My pet frog died," Tom croaked., "That dog's a mongrel," Tom muttered., "Answer the door," Tom chimed., "We've struck oil!" Tom gushed., "The campfire's hot enough," Tom bellowed., "We've have someone coming for supper?" tom guessed.

cronky: [paleologism] unsound, inferior

croodle: [paleologism] make low murmuring sound; huddle together, cower or crouch

Cropp's Law: The work accomplished's inversely proportional to the time available.

cross-nesting: story A evokes story B and vice versa

crossing: [David Frost] Hopalong casserole, Tarzan Stripe Forever

crot: [John Gardner] short, disconnected text separated by white space or asterisk

crowd: three-link chain of numbers whose factors add to each other

crowdle: [crow + croodle portmanteau] make low murmuring sound made by crows while huddling together, cowering or crouching

crustashun: [crustacean + shun portmanteau] person who cuts of the crust of their bread
crutches: [Bingo] seventy-seven, 77
cryptarithmetic: witty or factual statement provable by substituting numerals for letters: 2 x wrong = right, 3 x facet = whole, Brazil - trees = desert, pi x r^2 = area [Eric Le Vasseur], nine x four + five = forty-one [Leonard Gordon]
cryptonym: aka hidmid (hidden middle contraction), pseudonymous hiddenym between first/Christian and second/surname: Alan (Lana) Alda, Dale (Lee) Evans, Abraham (Hamlin) Lincoln, Mona (Ali) Lisa, Aristotle (Leon) Onasis, Omar (Masha) Sharif
cube: extrapolation of word square to three dimensions: CORD, OVER, RENO, DROP; OVER, VIVA, EVER, RARE; RENO, EVER, NEST, ORTS; DROP, RARE, ORTS, PEST
cubbered: [cupboard mondegreen] describes where one puts more than just cups
cubby-hole: [cubbyhole mondegreen] hiding place about the size of a teddy bear
cuephoria: [cue + euphoria portmanteau] joy when actor's long awaited signal to act finall comes
cull-de-sack: [cul-de-sac mondegreen] remove items from a bag or sack
cum hoc, ergo propter hoc: fallacy of false cause, see post hoc, ergo propter hoc
cummer: [cummerbund back-formation] any of various ingredients one might put into one's cummerbun
cumulative: round robin bouts rime with several poets taking turns
Curry's paradox: "If this sentence is true, then Santa Claus exists."
curtailable: word which remains a word or number which retains a propert after deletion of final letter or digit: like thirty-seven, which is prime like three
curtailment: operation of deleting final digit or dividing by ten and rounding, [n/10]
cuspodian: [cusp + custodian portmanteau] janitor trainee
cutless: [cutlass mondegeen] not-so-sharp knife
cryptarithm: substitution of letters for digits, similar to æquicalculus
cycle: see unicycle, bucycle, tricycle
cyclesomatic: [cycle + psychosomatic portmanteau] with thoughts of cycling in one's head
cyhydedd hir: [Welsh] quatrains with 2(3(5) + 4) = 38 syllables rhyming a^3b
cyhydedd naw ban: [Welsh] 9-syllable rhyme
cyrch a chwta: [Welsh] poem with 6(7) = 42 syllables rhyming a^4ba
cywydd: [Welch] 72-syllable rhyming couplet
cywydd llosgyrnog: [Welsh] poem with 2(2(8) + 7) = 46 syllables rhyming a^2bc^2b with midrhymes of a in 1st b, c in 2nd
cwot: [acronym] complete waste of time
D bait: [debate mondegreen] lure for the deadly D
d-invariant: word with d in 4th place: aardvark, aardwolf, abed, abidence, academia, acadia, aced, acidity, acidic, agedness, amidship, anode, aped, apodal, arid, auld, avidly, awed, ...
d-voiced: describes word whose d is turned to t: dab (tab), daffy (taffy), dale (tale), damp (tamp)
d'heuesque: [Mots d'heues + -esque] Anglo-French macaronic
daese: ["Dum anima est, spes esse." acronym] As long as there is life, there is hope.
daffynition: [daffy definition portmanteau] humorous meaning to word: battery: where bats live, bombard: bad poet, centimeter: what someone got from someone else expecting a female visitor, equipment: man's attempt at humor, gladiator: how cannibal felt about his mother-in-law, hijack: tool for putting on airplane tires, largess: S, locomotion: slight disturbance, mandate: male escort, pathologist: expert tracker, rhapsodist: store clerk at

Christmas, shamrock: artificial gemstone, stalemate: unresponsive spouse, sycophancy: what ails a hypochondriac

Dagari: describes words which change to another word when a double vowel with a d between is reduced to the vowel: Adam (am), biding (bing), chiding (ching), dodo (do), godown (gown), gradate (grate), odor (or), riding (ring), siding (sing), sliding (sling), see Af Jinni

damnesia: [damn + amnesia portmanteau] forgetfulness of condemnation

dandy lion: [dandelion mondegreen] especially attractive large male cat

dant: [dance back-formation] dance move, many of which make up a dance

darb: [paleologism] excellent

darble: [paleologism] fingerprint

daught: [daughter back-formation] what daughter does, akin to dote

davka: [Hebrew] because this is a fallen, imperfect world, not quite the same as stam

davrosism: [Davros of "Dr. Who"] exchange of the initial and final consonants of syllables or words, as Kaled to Dalek, as a secret language called Amagran

daw-daw: [paleologism] slow-witted

de-fender: [defender hyphenym] strip an automobile of its fenders

de-ooglification: substituting another sound for the oo-sound in googol (100^{50}): gogol (50^{50}), geegol (150^{50}), gorgol (200^{50}), fiegol (250^{50}), gigol (300^{50}), gegol (350^{50}), geigol (400^{50}), giengol (450^{50}), gengol (500^{50}), gelgol (550^{50}), gwelgol (600^{50}), girgol (650^{50})

deachnadh mor: [Irish] (86)2-syllabled rannaigheacht ending in 2-syllable words

dear: with seven, eight, or nine

dearer: with seven and eight or eight and nine or seven and nine

dearest: with seven and eight and nine

debious: ["Doesn't everyone believe it!" acronym back-formation] believing that another should believe that all others believe

deca: ["Dum excusare credis, accusas." acronym] When you believe you're excusing yourself, you're accusing yourself.

decadent: [deca- + dent] with only ten teeth left

decaffeilon: [decaffeinated + decathlon portmanteau] athletic competition in which not even caffeine is allowed

décima: [Span. "tenth"] 8-syllable-versed poem rhyming abbaaccdde

decimate: remove one (or every) tenth as in a sequence

decinary: referring to number system based on 10i, not 1/10

decor-rate: [decorate mondegreen] judge another's house furnishings

decompose: [mondegreen] edit a previously composed musical composition

deepenable: [dependable mondegreen] describing a well qualified lifeguard

defeatest: [defeatist mondegreen] describes someone most likely not to succeed

definism: fallacy of redefining terms to make it easier to defend

demigram: word whose front half and back are anagrams: horseshoer, intestines, reappear dental: d, d, t, t,

deportmanteau: divide portmanteau word into its constitutive elements

descenderless: letters or words without descenders (a, c, e, d, e, f, h, i, k, l, m, n, o, r, s, t, u, v, w, x, z): zero, one, two, three, four, five, six, seven, nine, ...

descrescendough: [decrescendo + dough portmanteau] when pastry collapses

dedil: [Dulce est desipere in loco. "It is sweet to relax at the proper time." acronym] timely R & R

deedeed: have offensive word, like "damned" bowdlerized to "d–: -d"

defriended: [friend in deed, friend indeed wordle] true friend

degeminated: describes word whose double letter is change to a single one: bee (be), beet (bet), boot (bot), coot (cot), loot (lot), too (to), toot, (tot), see ooglification

deletable: retaining property when a digit is deleted

delible: [indelible back-formation] able to be found at a delicatessen

deligate: [delegate mondegreen] gated entrance to a delicatessen

deliramental: pertaining to raving or foolish story

deliver: [de + liver] remove the liver from someone's body, full hepatectomy

delsda: ["Difficile est longum subito deponere amorem." (It is difficult to suddenly give up on love.) acronym] break-up trauma

demeaner: [demeanor mondegreen] peacemaker who decreases the meanness around him/her

DENEAT: [Michael Ecker] operation that transforms number by counting its "digits, even, not even and total", yielding 123 in a finite number of steps: googol = 10^{100} = 1001101 = 437 = 123 (3 steps), googolplex = 10^{googol} = 10^{201} + 10^{101} + 10^{100} + 1 = 1,974,201 = 347 = 123 (4 steps)

DeNever's Law: The simplest subjects are the ones you know nothing about.

density: ratio of a number's weight or sum of its digits, to its number volume

dennff: ["Deus et natua non faciunt frusta." acronym] God and nature do not work together in vain.

dentist: [-dd mondegreen] describes word ending in -dd like a dentist's name: add, hyperadd, odd, outadd, misadd, readd, rudd, sudd

denumerable: transfinites which are never-the-less able to be ordered, as in aleph-null, aleph-one (to-the-second-aleph-null), etc.

deossion: being buried alive

derling: [underling back-formation] well-to-do, upper class

des: ["Duco ergo sum." acronym] I calculate therefore I am.

description: transformation of number into a digit inventory, as 1 into 11, read as "one 1"

desipient: foolish

detqane: [Difficile est tenere quae acceperis nisi exerceas. acronym] It is difficult to retain what you may have learned unless you should practice it.

DeNever's Law: "The simplest subjects are the ones you know nothing about."

diacope: separation of compound word: never the less

diaersis: division of one syllable into two

dianoetical: logical

diatyposis: exciting language

dibious: ["D(on't) I b(elieve) i(t!)" acronym] believing that another should disbelieve that you believe

dice word: any of 420 4-letter words generated by throwing the four six-sided dice (AEIOTU, AEGHKO, BLPRST, CDMNRS)

didbious: ["D(isbelieve) I d(on't) b(elieve) i(t!)" acronym back-formation] believing that another should disbelieve that you do not believe

didious: ["D(on't) I d(isbelieve) i(t!)" acronym back-formation] believing that you disbelieve

die late: [dilate mondegreen] live a long life

difference word: [Dmitri Borgmann] word formed by taking the absolute value of the difference between a word's letter values as those of a new word: aft, en, I; boxty, mide, dea, ad

diffoccult: [difficult + occult portmanteau] hard to get others to believe in what they can't see, in the supernatural or yet undiscovered

digicharade: [digital charade portmanteau] word which has the same septemvigintary digits: love (12, 15, 22, 5) = above (1, 2, 15, 22, 5)

digincrement: [digitally increment portmanteau] increase each digit by one, as in transformation of 89 to 910

digipalindrome: word which has the same septemvigintary digits forward and backward: daemon (4, 1, 5, 13, 15, 14)

dihsch: [Dum inter homines sumus, colamus humanitatem.] As long as we are among humans, let us be humane.

dilapigate: [delapidate + gate portmanteau] old, broken-down entranceway

dillasegui: [looped illaseguid] poem with 7, 5, 5, 7, 5, 7, 5 = 36 syllables

dilling: [paleologism] youngest, smallest child or smallest animal of litter

dimensional dementia: [A. K. Dewdney] confusion of dimensions, as length for area or volume

Dingleus' number: ten-to-the-hundredth-to-the-ten-to-the-ten-thousandth-to-the-ten-to-the-hundredth, $(10^{100})^{\wedge}(10^{10,000})^{\wedge}(100)$

dimetre: [3 : 2 :: trimetre : ?] modified Alexandrine line with 12 syllables and caesara

dinoczar: [dinosaur + czar portmanteau] dictator who has outlived his time

dious: ["D(isbelieve) i(t!)" acronym back-formation] believing that another should disbelieve

diplogram: [J. H. Marshall] word with every letter repeated once: antianthropomorphisms, arraigning, esophagographers, happenchance, horseshoer, intestines, mama, murmur, papa, scintillescent, teammate, unsufficiences

dis-count: [dis(paragement) + count] keep track of the number of insults

disblessingguise: [blessing in disguise wordle] unrecognized blessing

disearning: [discern + earn portmanteau] complaining about how much you or someone else makes

disemvowelled: [disemboweled + vowel portmanteau] having had the vowels taken out: "dsmvlld" as in the so-called Bible Code, PRSVR Y PRFCT MN VR KP TS PRCPTS TN (Persevere ye perfect men; ever keep these precepts ten.)

disjunctive syllogism: always true logical statement, KCKApqNpqCKApqNqp

distance effect: difficulty in distinguishing two numbers increases as the distance between them, see Hamming distance

distichditope: [2 : p :: polytope : ?] polytope bounded by two hyperplanes: lune(digon), dihedron, etc.

divagation: act or process of wandering, straying, digressing, shifting or being incoherent, discursive, disconnected, incomprehensible, puzzling or unintelligent

divertisement: [divert + advertisement portmanteau] ad which is so entertaining that one can't remember what it was trying to sell

dixit: unconfirmed, sometimes dogmatic, statement

dizain: [Fren.] poem or number with 10(8 or 10) syllables

dogdancing: [paleologism] useless, exaggerated activity

dogdew: moisture on a dog's nose

dolly: [paleologism] excellent, very pleasant, attractive

domasticate: [domesticate + masticate portmanteau] trian a dog now to crew up everything
domisylum: [domicile + asylum portmanteau] madhouse
doppelgang: [doppelganger back-formation] couple of gangsters
doppelgänger: [Germ.] spirit of the not-yet dead, as in OOBEs
doppelgoogler: [doppelganger + google portmanteau] person who searches for others with same name
dom: ["Deo Optimo Maximo" acronym] to God, the Best, the Greatest
domino fallacy: claiming that one thing leads inevidiably to that argued against
domonym: name for people from certain location: Abarundi (Burundi), Angelenos (Los Angeles), Filipinos (Philippines), Liverpudlians (Liverpool), Oslovians (Oslo), Oxonians (Oxford), Quisqueyan (Dominican Republic), Wulfrunians (Wolverhampton)
Donsen's Law: The specialist learns more and more about less and less until, finally, he knows everything about nothing; whereas the generalist learns less and less about more and more until, finally, he knows nothing about everything.
doork: [door-dork portmanteau] person who pushes when the door says "pull" and pulls when the door says "push"
Doorkey Law: A person's status is equal to the number of doors that person can open divided by the number of keys needed, from those with keys without doors to those for whom doors are opened for them.
dothepe: [the inside dope wordle] insider information
double cross: word pair with shared central letter: (5) bring, flint; charm, meant; lunch, punch; sight, might; slate, train; (7) brother, flatter; condone, shudder; contend, whether; fashion, highest; immoral, rebound; pretend, weather; (9) charities, multitude; compiling, happiness; creatures, skeptical; dishonest, meteorite
doublet: [Lewis Carroll] aka word ladder [Dmitri Borgmann], laddergram, stepword, word golf, words pair, usually antonyms, linked by chain of words (rungs) differing by one letter: APE, apt, opt, oat, mat, MAN; BELL, ball, bale, bane, bang, bing, RING; BLACK, slack, stack, stalk, stall, stale, shale, whale, while, WHITE; BRIDE, brine, brink, crick, crock, crook, brook, broom, GROOM; CAT, cot, cog, DOG; CHECK, chick, chink, chins, COINS; HAND, hard, lard, lord, ford, fort, FOOT; HEAD, heal, teal, tell, tall, TAIL; POOR, boor, book, rook, rock, rick, RICH; WARM, ward, word, cord, COLD; TEARS, sears, stars, stare, stale, stile, SMILE
doublivore: [Grandville] two-headed creature, usually with one herbivorous and one carnivorous
doughnut: person obsessed with money
downpoor: [downpour mondegreen] financially challenged and depressed about it
doxastic: concerning belief state
drainchild: [braindrain + brainchild portmanteau] delinquent brainchild that drains rather than makes brainparent proud
dramadigit(s): [A. K. Dewdney] digit(s) beyond the last significant digit
dratt: [De Gerando acronym] "Decency renders all things tolerable."
Drazen's Law: The time to unfoul up a foul-up is inversely proportional to the time it took to foul up. (See Wolf's Law.)
dreerie: [dreary-eerie portmanteau] eerily dreary
droighneach: [Irish] poem with 9 13-syllable verses all with a3-syllable ending rhyming ababcdcd with crossrhymes and alliteration in each couplet
drongo: [paleologism] ugly fellow; lazy, undesirable; new recruit
droog: [paleologism] hooligan

dropalme: [pal-in-drome wordle] palindromic wordle

drøttkvaett: [Old Norse "bodyguard poem"] poem with 8 3-stressed verses with trochaic ending and internal rhyme

drub: [paleologism] deceive, befool, humbug

drumble: act sluggishly

druxy: semi-rotten, partially decayed

drydoc: [drydock mondegreen] physician who no longer drinks

ducks: [Bingo] twenty-two, 22

dudbious: ["D(isbelieve yo)u? Don't believe it!" grammanym back-formation] believing that another should not believe that they are not believed

dudownumps: [down in the dumps wordle] depressed

dudious: ["D(on't yo)u d(isbelieve) i(t!)" grammanym back-formation] believing that another should not disbelieve

duidecimal: [Dewey duodecimal mondegreen/portmanteau] referring to complex number system based on 12i

duff: [paleologism] ruin, render useless, no good; unreliable information

duffer: [paleologism] dull or stupid person

dungaree: [dungarer back-formation] one who is dungared by a dungarer

dungarer: [dungaree back-formation] one who dungars a dungaree

dunkle: [paleologism] something bad

Dunian: [Erdunian ard] with first three and last four lines unwritten

duzz: [Bingo from dozen] twelve, 12

dwaible: unstable

dwang: [paleologism] trouble

dye-it: [diet mondegreen] changing one's hair color to change one's looks rather than the more difficult losing weight

Dyer's Law: Paper flow produces more paper flow. (See Fowler's Law.)

dyfalu: [Welsh] succession of metaphors

dyitl: [Ps 37:4 acronym] "Delight yourself in the Lord."

Dykstra's Law: "Everybody's somebody's weirdo."

dyscalculic: [dyslexic analogue] able to calculate in reverse

dystopiary: [dystopia + topiary portmanteau] horrific, futuristic garden trimming

dyzzy: [from Douglas Hofstadter's dyz, dizzy answer to the analogy, abc : abd :: xyz : ?] "although insightful, so implausible and simple-minded as to invoke laughter"

e-invariant: word with e in 5th place: abase, abate, abide, abode, above, acumen, adage addle, adobe, adore, adoze, aerie, aether, afire, afore, afreet, agape, agate, agave, agaze, ...

E-keili: describes word with only e as a vowel: defense, defenseless, defenselessness, see, seek, seem

e-lipogram: text without the letter e: banana, primitivistic, polo, untrustful, syzygy

eac: ["Efructu arbor cognoscitur." acronym] The tree's known by its fruit.

eacol: ["Ex abundancia cordis, os loquitor." acronym] From the abundance of the heart the mouth speaks.

eafiwwitl: [Aesop acronym] "Even a fool is wise when it's too late."

ealphome: looped alphome, anagram with last letter moved to head

earing: [earring mondegreen] mistakenly putting something through one's ear

earmarxist: [earmark + Marxist portmanteau] socialist legislator who adds addendum to bill

earr: [ear + err portmanteau] mishear

earwane: [earwax antonym] deceasing of build-up in one's ear

Ebban: [Abbess Ebba of Coldington (d. c. 870), patron saint of palindromes] palindromic

echo poem: poem in the form of questions answered by echo of verse orstanza's last few words

eciamwow: [Disraeli acronym] "Everything comes if a man will only wait."

Eckenstrophe: [Middle High German] 12-line poem rhyming $a^2ba^2bcdcde^2$

eclectic chair: [eclectic + electric chair portmanteau] university position covering many different disciplines

ecnalg: [backward glance wordle] short look behind

Eddington's number: [Arthur Stanley Eddington] seventeen two-to-the-two-hundred-sixtieth

edging: erasing all but initial and final verses and initial and final words of other verses

Edison equation: genius = 1%(inspiration) + 99%(perspiration)

eek: [paleologism] face

eens: ["Extra ecclesiam nulla salus." acronym] Outside the Church [there's] no salvation.

eep: ["esse est percipi" acronym] to be is to be perceiving

efla: ["Eheu fugaces labuntur anni." acronym] Alas, the fleeting years slip by.

efregehefre: [ABCD : EFGH :: abracadabra : ?] nonsense word like abracadabra

eftilbaktof: [Youmans acronym] "Every fact that is learned becomes a key to other facts."

eggplant: [mondegreen] hide Easter eggs

eggsighting: [exciting mondegreen] finding Easter eggs during Easter egg hunt or spring birdwatching

eginagbagtag: [Demosthenes acronym] "Everything great is not always good, but all good things are great."

ego-boo: [ego boost, Frederick Pohl] whatever boosts one's ego

ehe: ["Errare humanum est." acronym] To err is human.

eheadment: [beheaded beheadment] double beheadment: brat, rat, at

ehhih: [Longfellow acronym] "Every human heart is Human."

eighty-eights: $8[10^{80}/9]$

eigne: [paleologism] eldest, firstborn

eitbos: [Carlyle acronym] "Experience is the best schoolmaster."

eiteos: [Arthur Helps acronym] "Experience is the extract of suffering."

either ore: [either or mondegreen] unspecified source of metals

ekka: [paleologism] exhibition

elbowroom: [elbow room mondegreen] storage room for prosthetic elbows

elc: [7LC (empathy) grammanym] empathetic level consciousness

electrinolosis: [electrolosis extrapolation] bombardment by neutrinoes

elemenym: [element + -nym] word transformable into another word by substitution of element name for symbol or vice versa: aged = silvered, fey = irony, hate = hydrogenate, nous = nitrogenous, Oates = oxygenates, set = sulfuret, sic = sulfuric, size = sulfurize

elementary: word with element letters: B (boron), C (carbon), F (flourine), H (hydrogen), I (iodine), K (potassium), N (nitrogen), O (oxygen), P (phosphorus), S (sulfur), U (uranium), V (vanadium), W (wolfram), Y (ytterbium): boon, chin, Confucius, finch, incubus, nippy, oops, phony, snoopy, soupy, subconscious, succubus, unconscious, vision, who, you

elemonate: [lemon + eliminate portmanteau] making a comment that sours an otherwise pleasant conversationio

elerate: [elevator acceleration portmanteau] mistakenly press an elevator button repeatedly, expecting that it will make it come faster

eletion: [beheaded deletion] transformation of word by deleting initial and one other letter: cache to ace

elev: ["Emitte Lucem et Veritatem." acronym] Send out Light and Truth

eleventy: [*The Hobbit* by J. R. R. Tolkien] eleven tens or one hundred ten, 11(10) = 110

elphomea: [plooed homealp with phonetic l-] alphabetic anagram with last six letters moved to head

ellogical: [beheaded "illogical" with phonetic l-] between logical and illogical

ellusionist: [beheaded illusionist with phonetic l-] between an illusionist and a lusionist

emaginary: [beheaded imaginary with syllabic m-] not quite 100% nonce words

emasculated: non-words in which the frag "man" is replaced by "person", "son/sun" by "child", "mail/male" by "letter": "Childday", "feletter", "letterperchild", "woperchild"

embarrister: [embarassed + barrister portmanteau] lawyer who loses his own case without any help from the opposition

emberdrome: [beheaded umberdrome with phonetic m-] doubly beheaded numberdrome

emiapwhil: [Plato acronym] "Every man is a poet when he's in love."

emitaohof: [Gallius Sallust acronym] "Every man is the architect of his own fortunes."

emmaterial: [beheaded immaterial with phonetic m-] between material and immaterial

emoat: [emote + moat] express joy at being surrounded by water

emohpla: [alphome ananym] zeewyexical anagram

emordnila: ["emordnila palindrome" palindrome] palindrome with nonce(s): "Smorael bats at times emit stable aromas.", "'Drowsi' is a word.", "'Tonsi' is also a word, but 'ubdrwaoslasi' is not.", "Neither is 'irehtien'."

emoticon: combiation of symbols to express emotions: :-) (smile) :-((frown) ;-) (wink) :-/ (half-smile) :-P (sticking out tongue)

empossible: [im/possible interpolation with verbalized m-] between possible and impossible

emprobable: [im/probable interpolation with verbalized m-] between probable and improbable

emtallage: metallage with first two letters exchanged, aka aangram

enallage: substitution of one grammatical form for another: noun for verb: "duck", "palm off"

enaveled: [enabled + navel portmanteau] with a newly cut and tied umbilical cord

encadenamento: [Span. "chaining together"] 1st verse of 2rd = 2nd verse of 3rd

endend: [end to end wordle] completely start to finish

endword: word formed from the ends of a bookend word: beer (betrayer), deer (debater), lint (ligament), my (money), rent (resident)

enfinite: [nfinity with phonetic n-] between finite and infinite surreal numbers

engine ear: [engineer mondegreen] skill for recognizing trouble under the hood just from the sound

englyn: [Welsh] poem with 10 + 6 + 2(7) 30 syllables rhyming ab^3

Enian: [beheaded Unian with phonetic n-] with first five and last four lines unwritten

enigmoid: puzzle that begins like an enigma but ends with obvious answer: "What did one carrot say to the other?" "Nothing, because carrots can't talk.", "Who was Julius Caesar's great-grandfather?" Nemo Scit ("Nobody knows.")

enjambemement: when one verse runs on to next

enloopu: [unloop unloop with phonetic n-] form (21, 231, 2341, etc.) anagrams by moving initial letter to tail

enrationals: [phonetically spelled nrationals] nverted unrationals

ensics: [forensics back-formation] study of the detective's analysis after the mystery is solved

entelligence: [phonetically spelled ntelligence] between intelligence and telligence

enversion: [beheaded inversion with phonetic n-, 1/x : inversion :: 1\x : ?] mathematical operation symbolized by the backslash that turns a decimal on its radix
eodermdrome: [Gary Bloom, John Kennedy, Peter Wexler] word with crossed connectors in its word graph: nonplanar, forethoughtfulness, overconcentration, pseudohermaphroditism, saponaceousness, unadulteratedness, unconscientiousnessenthymene: argument with part understood
eotar: [Mt 7:8a acronym] "Every one that asks receives."
epanados: repetition of word or phrase at beginning and middle or middleand end
epanalepsis: ending as begun: "I would like that, would I."
epanorthosis: [Greek "setting straight again"] correction
epenthesis: inserting a letter, phoneme or syllable into a word: "famdamily", "visitating"
epignostic: [epi- + gnostic compound] having knowledge beyond the pseudo-knowledge of the gnostics
Epimenides paradox: aka Liar's paradox, self-referential "All Cretans are liars." by Epimenides or non-referential by Paul (Ti 1:12-13), see Ultimate Law
epimythium: moral at end of fable
epistrophed: with endword repeated
epizeuxis: repetition for emphasis
Epongliposh: opposite of Turkey Irish, English with -po- after vowels, aka closed Glopish [Openglopish back-formation]
eponym: word from a proper name: America (Amerigo Vespucci), americium (America), ammonia (Jupiter Ammon), amp (André, Marie Ampere, aphrodisiac (Aphrodite), artesian (Artois, France), atlas (Atlas), August (Augustus Caesar), baloney (Bologna), bayonet (Bayonne, France), bedlam (St. Mary of Bethlehem Hospital, London), berkelium (Berkeley, Cal.), bloomers (Amelia Jenks Bloomer), caesarean (Julius Caesar), californium (California), caracul (Karakul), cashmere (Kashmir), catamite (Ganymede),cereal (Ceres), cologne (Cologne), columbium (Christopher Columbus),cravat (Hrvat or Croatian), cupidity (Cupid), curium (Pierre and Marie Curie), currant (Corinth), derby (Derby, Eng.), dollar (Joachimstal), echo, einsteinium (Albert Einstein), erbium (Ytterby, Sweden), ermine (Armenia), erotic (Eros), Europe (Europa), europium(Europe), fermium (Enrico Fermi), francium (France), frankfurter (Frankfurt, Germ.), Friday (Frigg), gadolinium (Johan Gadolin), gallium(Paul ⬚mile Lecoq de Boisbaudran), gardenia (Alexander Garden), gargantuan (Gargantua), gat (R. J. Gatlin), germanium, guillotine (Dr. Joseph I. Guillotin), gun (Gunnhildr), hackney (Hackney, Eng.), hafnium (Hafnia aka Copenhagen, Denmark), hamburger (Hamburg, Germ.),hermetically (Hermes), holmium (Stockholm, Sweden), indigo (India), indium (India), iris (Iris), jovial (Jove), July (Julius Caesar),lawrencium (Ernest Orlando Lawrence), lilliputian (Lilliput), limo(Limousin, France), lutetium (Lutetia or Paris, France), magnesium (Magnesia), manganese (Magnesia), magnet (Magnesia), marcel (Marcel Grateau), martial (Mars), maudlin (Mary Magdalene), mayonnaise (McMahon), meander (Maeander River, Phrygia), mendelevium (Dmitri Mendelev), mho(Georg Simon Ohm), milliner (Milan, Italy), mohole (A. Mohorovicic), moron (Moron), nemesis (Nemesis), neptunium (Neptune), New Jersey(Caesar), nickel (St. Nicholas), nicotine (Jean Nicot), nobelium (Alfred Nobel), ogre (Orcus), ohm (Georg Simon Ohm), palladium (Pallas), panic (Pan), parchment (Pergamum), peach (Persia), petrel (St. Peter), pistol (Pistoia, Italy), plimsoll (Samuel Plimsoll), plutonium (Pluto), poinsettia (Joel Roberts Poinsett), polka (Poland), polonium (Poland), poo-bah (Pooh-Bah), praline (César de Choiseul, mar, chal du Plessis-Praslin, protean (Proteus), quixotic (Don Quixote), rhenium (Rhine River), rhinestone (Rhine River), ruthenium (Ruthenia or

Russia), samarium (M. von Samarski), sandwich (John Montagu, fourth Earl of Sandwich), Saxophone (Antoine J. Sax), Saturday (Saturn), scandium (Scandinavia), selenium (Selene), shrapnel (Lt. Henry Shrapnel), spaniel, spinach, spruce (Prussia), strontium (Strontian, Scotland), suede(Sweden), tangerine (Tangiers), tantalum (Tantalus), tantony (St. Anthony), tarantula (Taranto, Italy), tawdry (St. Audrey), terbium (Ytterby, Sweden), thorium (Thor), thulium (Thule), Thursday (Thor), titanium (Titan), Tuesday (Tiu), uranium (Uranus), valentine (St. Valentine), vanadium (Vanadis), venereal (Venus), volt (Count Alessandro Volt), vulcanize (Vulcan), watt (James Watt), Wednesday (Woden), ytterbium (Ytterby, Sweden), yttrium (Ytterby, Sweden)

Epstein's Law: "An unsolved problem is bad, but a 'solved' problem is worse."

epu: ["e pluribus unum" acronym] from many one

equalotry: [equality + -alotry portmanteau] worship of "equality"

equiliteral: with the same number of letters in number name as another number name:one, two, six, ten; four, five, nine

equiprobability: principle by which opposites alternate potentiality and actuality: day and night, odds and evens

equivalency: set of number names that demonstrate some kind of equality

Z	E	R	O	+	N	I	N	E	=	9
O	N	E	+	E	I	G	H	T	=	9
T	W	O	+	S	E	V	E	N	=	9
T	H	R	E	E	+	S	I	X	=	9
F	O	U	R	+	F	I	V	E	=	9

equivoque: text able to be read in two different ways: "I shall waste no time reading the book you gave me.", "If you come within ten miles of my home, pray stop there."

Er: [Manx Ero] poem doubly curtailed, reversed and then triply curtailed

eraslings: [eraser + sling + -lings portmanteau] small bits of remnants of used rubber esasure that tend to fly in every direction

Erdunian: [beheaded Verdunian] with first and last four lines unwritten

Ero: [Manx Eroo] poem doubly curtailed, reversed and then doubly curtailed again

Eroo: [Manx Eroom] poem doubly curtailed, reversed and then curtailed again

Eroom: [Percy Moore] poem doubly curtailed and then reversed

erroar: [error + roar portmanteau] much to do about a little mistake

error, close: error that is almost not, "Close only counts in horseshoes."

error, communative: error in applying communative law, such as n/n' = n'/n

error, dimensional: error in dimensions or units, $n^2 \approx n^3$, $(\$10)^2 \approx \$100$

error, distributive: error in applying distributive law, such as $(n + n')^2 = n^2 + n'^2$

error, magnitude or scale: error caused by mistaking a magnitude, such as $n^{3.0} \approx n^{30}$, million $\approx$ billion

error, name-thing: [Jean Piaget] mistaking name for thing or vice versa

error, operand: error caused by misremembering rote learning

error, operational: error caused by misunderstanding operation

error, pigs-is-pigs: [Ellis Butler] mistaking meaning of words, such as Guinea pigs = pigs from Guinea

ertia: [inertia back-formation] movement
espinella: [Vincent Espinel] poem with 10 8-syllable lines rhyming $ab^2a^2c^2d^2e$
etar: [Plato acronym] "Excellent things are rare."
ethicalculus: [ethical calculus portmanteau] any process that evaluates alphadigital strings as numbers, as in base twenty-seven, base thirty-six
euphuism: [John Lyly's *Euphues*] excessively rhetorical, figurative or mythological, like: for humorous effect: in *The Sot-Weed Factor* by John Barth
evener: with an even number of prime factors
eventide: [mondegreen] even hours of the day
evenum: number with all even digits
evenym: [even letter word] vowelless word with only the even letters (b, d, f, g, j, l, n, p, r, t, v, x, z): brr, DLXV, grr, nth, phfft, xth, zzzz
everywear: [everywhere mondegreen] clothing that can be wore in every occasion
evitable: [inevitable back-formation] uncertain, dubious
evitpol: [acronym] "Eternal vigilance is the price of victory."
ewhaw: [Shakespeare acronym] "Every why hath a wherefore."
ex-aisle: [exile mondegreen] section of a store that has become block by restocking the shelves
ex-citation: [excitation hyphenym] fragments of torn-up traffic ticket
ex-ile: [exile hyphenym] sunken island like Atlantis or Lemuria
ex-porter: [exporter hyphenym] former baggage carrier
ex-pouration date: [expiration date mondegreen] date at which a bottled liquid shouldnot be poured
ex-press: [express hyphenym] former reporter
ex-tent: [extent hyphenym] canvas formerly used as a temporary dwelling
ex-terminator: [exterminator hyphenym] reprogrammed killer robot
ex-tradition: [extradition hyphenym] something that once was customarily done
ex-word: back-formation from word beginning with ex-
ex-xylophone: xylophone that has been broken up into individual chimes
exa: [8 : mega :: 20 : ?] two-to-the-twentieth = 2^{20} = 1,048,576
examnesia: [exam amnesia portmanteau] memory lost experience during an examination
excessorize: [excessive accesorize portmanteau] add too many items to one's apparel
exclusionary: sharing no digits with its base, as in exclusionary cube
existential affirmative: Kpq
existential negative: KpNq
existron: [mega : exa :: megistron : ?] to-the-twentieth-two = $^{20}10$
Exna: [Manx with phonetic x-] curtailed, reversed then curtailed again
Exnam: [Percy Manx with phonetic x-] curtailed and then reversed
exonym: word used by foreigners, not that used by natives: Cologne (Köln), Florence (Firenze), Morocco (Maroc), Moscow (Moskva)
expectherent: [expectorant mondegreen] describes landlords
explosive: b, d, g, k, p, t
exponential: combinatorial literature of the form n^n: *Cent Mille Milliards de Poèmes* by Raymond Queneau's 10^{14} sonnets
extraordinary: [Pierre Simon de LaPlace] with a probability of at most a millionth (microkan), $P \le 10^{-6}$
extravagant: integer whose with factorization less than itself, not prime or frugal

Exxonerated: [Exxon + exonerated portmanteau] given reduced sentence because of big business employer

eye-rhyme: heteronymous rhyme that looks like it should sound like previous word but doesn't

f-invariant: word with f in 6th place: acetify, acidify, airlift, alewife, amplifier, angelfish, beatific, behalf, behoof, belief, bellyful, blissful, boastful, engulf, hereof, ingulf, itself, khalif, massif, ...

Faber's Laws: (1) If there isn't a law, there will be. (2) The number of errors in any piece of writing rises proportionately to the writer's reliance on secondary sources. (3) "We're all going down the same road in different directions." (4) Necessity is the mother of strange bedfellows.

fablo: [D'ni] twenty-five-to-the-fifth, not-so-little tenplex, $25^5 = 5^{10} = 9,765,625$

factorial: product of numbers from 1 to n, symbolized by n!; work wherein elements may be permutated in n! ways as in 17th century protean poetry: "Honor, art, money, property, praise, woman and child one has, seeks, misses, hopes for, and disappears." (*Récréations* by G. P. Harsdörffer)

factorion: [R. Dougherty] equal to sum of individual digits' factorials, (of the second kind, near-factorion) sum of all but all but one digit, (of the third kind) product of grouped digits' factorials

faff: [paleologism] wasting time when there's an urgent need

Fagari: describes words which change to another word when a double vowel with an f between is reduced to the vowel: befell (bell), bifid (bid), refed (red), safari (sari), wifing (wing), see Af Jinni

faint praise: [mondegreen] laudatory comment of delicate Victorian ladies

fair-in-height: [Fahrenheit mondegreen] of only average stature

Fairfax's Law: [fair facts] Any facts which, when included in the argument, give the desired result, are fair facts for the argument.

fake: smallest positive integer greater than predecessor consistent with sequence

fakon: [fake bacom portmanteau] meatless bacon-flavored bits served at salad bars

false analogy: overemphasizing what two things have in common, while ignoring differences

false dilemma: fallacy of implying that if p or q is true and q is not then p is, CKApqNqp

false hood: [falsehood mondegreen] gang infiltrator, undercover policeman/woman

false negative: positive erroneously counted as negative test result

false positive: negative erroneously counted as positive test result

famel: [D'ni] twenty-five-to-the-fourth, not-so-little eightplex, $25^4 = 5^8 = 390,625$

far: long, long way to run

fara: [D'ni] twenty-five-squared, $25^2 = 5^4 = 625$

farpotshket: [Yiddish] potential fubar (foul-up beyond all recovery), aka pfubar, not quite the same as Schlimmbesserung

fasfi: [Emerson acronym] "Fear always springs from ignorance."

fast: [Alain René Le Sage acronym] "Facts are stubborn things."

fat-headed: [fatheaded hyphenym] describing a word beginning with fat- but not referring to fat: fatal, fatale, fate, father, fatherhood, fathom, fatigue

fatrasie: [Fren. "medley, rubbish"] 11-versed macaronic poem

fauxho: [faux + hole portmanteau, ≈ moho] phony holes on speaker covers, put there to match the ones that actually surround the speaker

featherb: [featherbed back-formation] stuff with feathers

feen: [Joseph Bowden] 15 (base 10) in base 16

feenominal: [fee + phenomenal portmanteau] for minimal cost

fehomi: ["Forsan et haec olim meminisse iuvabit." acronym] Perhaps even this will one day be pleasant to look back on.

feminine: describes 2-syllabled endrhyme

feminization: turning masculine endrhyme into feminine by doubling last syllable

feminym: [feminine + -nym] M2F (male-to-female) pseudonym: Crystal Croftangley (Sir Walter Scott), Mrs. Silence Dogoody (Benjamin Franklin), Razilee Mary Purdue (Michael Joseph Halm), Dorothea Julia Ramsbottom (William Makepeace Thackery), Fiona MacLeod (William Sharp)

fenderberg: [fender iceburg portmanteau] large glacial deposits that form on the undersides of car fenders during snowstorms

feoc: ["Fames est optimus coquus." acronym] Hunger is the best cook.

fericomplexority: [in-feriority complex wordle] inferiority complex

Fermat: two-to-a-power-of-two plus one, $F_n = g(2, 2^n, 2) + 1$

fernish: [furnish mondegreen] somewhat like a fern

Fetridge's Law: Important things that are supposed to happen don't, especially when others are watching.

fewchsia: [few + fuchsia portmanteau] rare, purplish-red flower

fewteen: [Pol. kilkanaście] in lower teens, 13 to 15

fewty: [fewteen extrapolation] in lower tens, 10 to 40

fibonym: [Fibonacci + -nym portmanteau] word with just Fibonacci letters (a, b, c, e, h, m, u): ace, bum, chum, each, much

fibonaccian: split into n discontiguous elements to produce Fibonacci's number, $F(n) = 1 + n!/(1!(n-1)) + (n-1)!/(2!(n-3)) + ...$, of combinations

fif: ["Fabas indulcet fames." ("Hunger sweetens the beans.") acronym] hunger is the best sauce

fifatre: [fat in fire] sometime that makes situation more intense, more uncontrollable

fiff: [fif(teen)]: 15 or 15/60 or quarter past hour

fifty-fives: 55,555,555,555,555,555,555,555,555,555,555,555,555,555,555,555,555 = $5[10^{50}/9]$

filthynym: [back-formation] aka tic-tac-toe board word, with only letters with horizontal and/or vertical lines (F, H, I, L, T): fill, filth, flit, hi, hill, hilt, hit, I, if, iff, ill, it, lift, lit, til, till, tilt, tit

finally: with only ten steps left to go

Finagle's Laws: (1) If an experiment works, something has gone wrong. (2) No matter what the experiment's result, there will always be someone eager to: (a) misinterpret it. (b) fake it. or (c) believe it supports his own pet theory. (3) In any collection of data, the figure most obviously correct, beyond all need of checking, is the mistake. (4) Once a job is fouled up, anything done to improve it only makes it worse.

Finangle's Rule: (6) "Don't Believe in miracles; depend on them!"

Finnegan's Law: "The further away the future, the better it looks."

Finnigan's Law: "That which is most obviously correct, beyond all apparent need to check, is the mistake."

fireproof: [homonym] unable to be fired, with tenure

firsim: [Fortiter in re, suaviter in modo. acronym] Resolutely in action, gently in manner; do unhesitatingly what must be done, but accomplish it as inoffensively as possible.

fisseliger: [German] person flustered to the point of distraction by an unwanted and not-so-helpful kibitzer or nagging supervisor

fitcor: [William Adams acronym] "Faith is the continuation of reason."

fitfol: [Tolstoy acronym] "Faith is the force of life."
FitzGibbon's Law: Creativity's inversely proportional to the number of cooks involved with the broth. (See Kirkland's Law.)
fiufio: ["Falsus in uno, falsus in omnibus." acronym] False in one thing, false in all
five-headed: word beheadable five times before becoming a non-word: eastern, growing
flamp: [paleologism] flatter, wheedle
flate: [de/inflate back-formation] un/fill with air or other gas
fledg: [fledgling back-formation] mature bird
fleer: [paleologism] word or look of derision or mockery
flop: [fantasy left out personality acronym] someone who has no daydreams and so cannot have dreams come true
flopcorn: [flop + popcorn portmanteau] unpopped popcorn kernels
fluezy: [flu + floozy portmanteau] woman prone to getting influenza because of all the men she makes contact with
flumdiddle: [paleologism] polite nonsense
flyte: [paleologism] exchange insults
follygraph: [folly + polygraph] record of one's youthful folly (meng)
fonddo: [fond + hairdo portmanteau, ≈ fondue] favorite hair style
foolosopher: [fool + philosopher portmanteau] foolish philosopher or philosophic fool
foolscape: [fool + landscape portmanteau, ≈ foolscap] where all that one can see is foolishness
fooniferism: [foonerism + kniferism portmanteau] switching of non-clustered final and initial consonants and initial vowel clusters, as "defghij" to "jifghed"
for'um: [forum mondegreen] what you are when you're not ag'in 'um
fore-headed: [forehead hyphenym] describing a word beginning with fore- not referring to fore-: foreign, foreignborn, foreigner, forensics, forester, forestry
forkerism: [spoon : spoonerism :: fork : ?] exchange of final consonant clusters of syllables or words, as "defghij" to "dejghif"
forkniferism: [forkism + knifism portmanteau] switching both final consonant and vowel clusters, as "defghij" to "dijghef"
formenstahlen: [Germ.] energy associated with shape
fornyrdhislag: [Old Norse] 4-versed poem with caesura, each half-verse with alliteration, 2 stressed syllables and 2 or 3 unstressed
forword: pure word with letters from the front half of the alphabet, a-to-m: hammamelidaceae
four: [fore homonym] exclamation when about to count beyond three
four cross: four words sharing end letter pairs, 2 as initials, 2 as finals: b<u>ad</u>, <u>da</u>y, <u>ad</u>d, m<u>ad</u>; <u>ma</u>r, <u>pa</u>r, <u>ra</u>t, <u>ra</u>w
four-headed: word beheadable four times before becoming a nonword: astern, cheat, rowing, score, scram, spore, there, where, woman
fourage: [four + forage portmanteau] search for fours
fourfather: [forefather mondegreen] any of a person's four great grandfathers
fourmother: [foremother mondegreen] any of a person's four great grandmothers
fourparent: either forefather or formother
foursite: [foresight mondgreen] position, if any, of the digit four in a number
fourty-fours: 4,444,444,444,444,444,444,444,444,444,444,444,444 = $4[10^{40}/9]$
fractorial: [Charles Douglas Wehner] factorial of fraction, $\Pi(n/n' + 1)$
frag: [frag of "fragment"] partial word, used in forming frag networks, see teau,

Franglish: "Pas de leur aune que nous." (Paddle your own canoe.)

Franklin's corollary to Comin's Law: People will not accept your idea more readily if you tell them Comins said it first.

fratrinym: [brothered word] word beginning with br-, generating a fictitious name, Br. A, Br. Ace, Br. Agger, Br. Ed, Br. Ian, Br. Ink, Br. East, Br. Oad, Br. Oken

fraznit: [frazzle + knit portmanteau] thread or yarn hanging from an article of clothing which when pulled causes the article to unravel

freedumb: [freedom + dumb portmanteau] dumb enough to believefreedom is free, that it means getting free stuff

Freeman's Law: Nothing is so simple it cannot be misunderstood.

Fredkin's paradox: The more similar two choices are, the more time a decision-making agent spends on deciding.

Freitag's triangle: the pattern of introduction, rise in conflict, climax, fall and denouement

fricatives: f, s, v, z

fricky: [paleologism] nervously irritated, on-edge

fribble: [paleologism] act frivolously; one who is frivolous

frigenetics: [refrigerator + genetic portmanteau] experimental pseudoscience of returning to the refrigerator in hopes that something new will have spontaneously generated

friggypoo: [paleologism] pretentious nonsense

friendlier: describes friendly word whose replaced letters also are a word: bane = pane, bone, bare, bank = pork

friendliest: describes word in which every substitution of a letter or combination of letters forms a garble group of other words: bane = mane, bine, bate, bant, mine, mate, mant, bite, bint, batt, mite, mint, matt, bitt

friendly: describes word (olanosi) in which the substitution of each of its letters generates another word: bane = lane, bone, bade, bank

friwaftt: [Pope acronym] "Fools rush in where angels fear to tread."

fron: [Joseph Bowden] 14 (base 10) in base 16

fuelogy: [fuel + eulogy portmanteau] prediction of or lamentation over a fuel shortage

fuhror: [Feuher + furor portmanteau] uproar over Nazism or neo-Nazism

fukashigi: [Jap.] ten-to-the-sixty-fourth, sixty-fourplex, 10^{64}

fukashigigasha: [kou : kougasha :: fukashigi : ?] ten-to-the-eighty-fourth, 10^{84}

fulfill: fill with filling until what is not full is full, but not too fully filled

funnelvision: [funnel + tunnelvision portmanteau] ability to focus, even over-focus

furph: [paleologism] false report

futurology: [Theodor Rossak] religious: Judeo-Christian, Neopaganism, Occult, Oriental cult revivals; bioenergetics and martial arts, eupsychiatrics, macrobiotics, Oriental therapies, pop culture, psychics, psychotronics, wild science

fuv: ["Fac ut vivas." acronym] Get a life

fuzzy logic: [Zadeh] logic using hedges (almost, almost certainly, almost not, more-or-less, nearly, nearly not, not possibly, not very, possibly, probably, rather, slightly, somewhat, very possibly) and qualifiers (few, many, most, several...)

Fyfe's Laws: (1) Information necessitating a change in plans will be communicated to the planner after: and only after: the plans are complete. (2) The more innocuous the change in plans appears the great the change will actually be. (3) It is always simpler to start over from scratch than make changes in a plan already started. (4) The more carefully and painstakingly a sample is analyzed the greater the probability it will be found irrelevant.

g-devoiced: describes a word whose g is changed to a k phoneme: gam (cam), gap (cap), gat (cat), goat (coat), gut (cut)

g-invariant: word with g in 7th place: amazing, aerology, agrology, alienage, although, amperage angling, antilog, apothegm, archange, archings, areology, arisings, asparagus, ...

g-whiz: [gee whiz mondegreen] gravitonics expert

Gagari: describes words which change to another word when a double vowel with a g between is reduced to the vowel: liege (lie), logo (lo), rigid (rid), see Af Jinni

gai: [Jap.] ten-to-the-twentieth, twentyplex, 10^{20}

gaita-gallega: [Span. "Galician bagpipe"] poem or number with 11 syllables

galah: [paleologism] simpleton, fool

Galileo's paradox: Though most numbers are not squares, there are no more numbers than squares

Gall's Law: [John Gall] A complex system that works invariably evolved from a simple system that also did.

galmadri: [oploed madrigal] poem rhyming (aa)aabcdbcd(bcd) or (a)abcbcac(bcaa)

gammagon: [gamma + -gon] polygon formed from gamma-like right angles, including two-gamma square, three-gamma irregular hexagon, four-gamma concave irregular hexagon, five-gamma stellated pentagon

gan: [Sino-Korean] ten-to-the-thirty-sixth, thirty-sixplex, 10^{36}

gananagati: [Sanskrit] ten-to-the-forty-first, forty-oneplex, 10^{41}

Gapland: [gap + Lapland portmanteau] boundary-less land between the "You are now leaving" and "You are now entering" signs

garb age: [garbage charade] how old one's wardrobe is

garmite: [garment + mite portmanteau] clothing that fit perfectly in the store, but somehow became much smaller on the way home

gator aide: [gatorade mondegreen] alligator's personal assistant

gatsalts: [Aesop acronym] "Grasp the shadow and lose the substance."

gaugeous: [gauge + gorgeous portmanteau] having beautiful measurements

gayatri: [Sanskrit] poem or number with 24 syllables

gazumph: [paleologism] swindle; short change

geeography: [gee + geography portmanteau] especially impressive landscape photography

geishous: [geisha + gaseous] describing almost invisible geisha-like servant

gelogenics: art and science of provoking laughter

geminated: describes words with letters doubled: be (bee), bet (beet), bot (boot), cot (coot), lot (loot), to (too), see ooglification

general: [gen- mondegreen] describes word beginning with gen- generating a fictitious name, Gen. Eric, Gen. Eticist, Gen. Ius, Gen. Ocidal, Gen. Tile, Gen. Uine

generalization: [mondegreen] process of promoting someone to the rank of general

gentillion: [nongentillion back-formation] not ten-to-the-two-hundred-seventy-third, $\neq 10^{273}$)

geo-metrics: [Gerald Lynton Kaufman's Geo-Metric Verse] includes barrel-lyric, cubicouplet, ellipsonnet, pastor-lel-ogram, rhombucolic, right-triangolet, rounderlay, sine-curverse, sphere-rondeau, squarodyghazal

Gerrold's Law: A little ignorance can go a long way.

Gershwin's Law: [George Gershwin] It ain't necessarily so.

geuk: [Sino-Korean] ten-to-the-forty-eighth, forty-eightplex, 10^{48}

ghost: [W. W. Skeat] nonword accidentally listed in dictionary, etc.: Dord

ghotism: [from Bernard Shaw's "ghoti"] antiphonetic spelling in which f = gh, ff, ft, ph, pph, ugh (enough, off, soften, physics, sapphire, laugh), i = ai, e, ee, ei, ia, o, u, ui, y (villain, pretty, been, forfeit, marriage, women, busy, guilt, hymn), sh = ce, chsi, psh, sci, sch, si, ss, ti (ocean, fuchsia, pshaw, conscience, schwa, pension, issue, nation), yielding 432 spelling for "fish"

giapjoiti: [Victor Hugo acronym] "Genius is a promontory jutting out into the infinite."

gib: [paleologism] gal/guy in back navigating

Gibberish: substituting neighboring letter in typewriter order: "Honnrtodj" or "Fuvvweuag"

giddy-upper: [giddy-up back-formation] upper that has the side-effect of making one giddy

gif: [paleologism] gal/guy in front piloting

giga: [8 : mega :: 11 : ?] two-to-the-eleventh, little elevenplex = 2^{11} = 2,048

gigantic: with at least a hundred thousand digits, $\log(n) \geq 5$

gigillion: [gig(a)- + -illion] ten-to-the-three-million-third, three-million-threeplex = $10^{3,000,000,003}$

gigastron: [mega : giga :: megistron : ?] to-the-eleventh-two = $^{11}2$

gigawc: [Owen Meredith acronym] "Good-humor is goodness and wisdom combined."

Gil: [acronym] "God is love. "

Gilbalmead: [balm in Gilead wordle] panacea

ginch: [paleologism] elegence, smartness in skills, manners or dress

gink: [paleologism] look

gioras(avphit): [Ps 47:1 acronym] "God is our refuge and strength, a very present help in trouble."

giraffiti: [graffiti + giraffe portmanteau] graffiti above eye-level to make it more difficult to remove

gister: [register back-formation] take a superficial first look without noticing what ought to be noticed

gitalhs: [Plato acronym] "God is truth and light His shadow."

gith: [Spurgeon acronym] "Giving is true having."

glad'e-ate-'er: [gladiator mondegreen] attitude of an unrepentant cannibal

glibido: [glib + libido portmanteau] passionate talkativeness

gleek: [paleologism] joke, tease, taunt

glerint: [Ferengi] twelve-to-the-fourth, square gross, 12^4 = 20,736

gleitender: [Germ.] describes 3-syllable rhyme

glocken: [glockenspiel back-formation] salesman whose sales pitch is mere noise

glom: pronouncable pseudo-word as in scrabble or anagrams, compare with zyxnoid

Glopish, Closed: [Openglopish (Turkey Irish) antonym] secret language formed by adding -po- after vowels, aka Ireland Turkish

glosa: [Span.] introductory cabeza with glossing stanzas

gneed: [need back-formation] want that's misperceived as a need

gnibbur: [back rubbing wordle] massaging of back

gnomic: [gnomon "complimentary shape"] first differences of

gnoming: [paleologism] studying, not partying

goadee: [goad back-formation, $\approx$ goatee] one being encouraged or persuaded to go on

goby: [paleologism] go-between

Godincidence: [God coincidence portmanteau] small miracle

godspeed: instantaneous because

goggler: [paleologism] television addict

goku: [Jap.] ten-to-the-forty-eight, forty-eightplex, 10^{48}

Goliath: power of two with 666 "666" frags
golth: [goth + golf portmanteau] early outdoor sport involving putting little black balls into holes in the ground
gongorrhea: [Gongorism + gonorrhea] chronic obscurancy
goober: one who goobs, that is, eats peanuts
Goodfader's Law: The few who are best will better the rest.
goog: [paleologism] simpleton, fool; egg
googoc: twenty-to-the-two-hundredth, 20^{200}
googol: [Milton Sirotta] ten-to-the-hundredth, hundredplex, twoduplex, 10^{100}
googologism: word or phrase, such as googol for ten-to-the-hundredth or great googol for ten-to-the-thousandth, used as informal number names for large numbers
googologue: dissertation of googology, especially a long and confusing one in idiomatic nomenclature
googology: [googo- + -ology] branch of number theory dealing with googols, googolplexes and related large, yet finite numbers
googolplex: [Edward Kasner] ten-to-the-googolth, 10^{googol}
googomania: obsessive, compulsive googolologizing
googonaut: a lurker or fan of googology without actually being a googologist
googophiliac: person who loves large numbers, see googonaut, googologist
googophobia: variety of math anxiety manifesting as fear of large numbers
googoscopic: combining art and science together via googology
googosophy: the philosophy of large numbers, including the syntactic and the abstract branches
gorasavphit: [acronym] "God's our Refuge and Strength, a very present Help in trouble."
Gordon's First Law: A project that isn't worth doing at all isn't worth doing well.
gorm: [paleologism] chewing tobacco; stare long and greedily; chewing tobacco
gormless: [paleologism] stupid, slow-witted, lacking common sense
gosbom: [Homer acronym] "Gentle of speech, beneficent of mind."
gossling: [gosling mondegreen] what a gossler does, not quite as noisy as guzzling
Grabel's Law: [Arvand Grabel] "Two does not equal three, even for very large values of two."
grafootve: [one foot in grave] nearly dead
grammanym: [letter word] word (or phrase) expressible as acronymic homonym: anemone (NMNE), are (R), be, bee (B), be seein' you (BCNU), cue (Q), cutie (QT), devious (DVS), empty (MT), enemy (NME), essay (SA), ex (X), excellency (XLNC), expediency (XPDNC), obediency (OBDNC), okay (OK), pea (P), see (C), tea (T), you (U), why (Y)
grandower: [grandeur + power portmanteau] quality of being not only grand but also powerful
granduation: [grand + graduate portmanteau] when an older-than-average student finally completes their education
graphics: techniques of plotting letter connections in words, including C-graph, H-graph, K-graph, OS-graph, Q-graph, R-graph, T-graph, symbolized by letter prefix and parentheses enclosing the sequence of each alphabeticalized letter's number of connections: arm = (1, 1,2), area = (2, 2, 2), banana = (2, 1, 1), going (2, 2, 2, 2), people (3,2, 2, 3); the graph is traversable exactly once if at most two letters have odd number of connections
grasnakess: [snake in the grass wordle] hidden danger
great: [great gross back-formation] -to-the-three-halvesth, $n^{3/2}$
gred: [blue : grue :: red : ?] green, like a leaf which will be turning red in Fall or traffic like that turns from green to red

grellow: [blue : grue :: yellow : ?] green, of a leaf which will be turning yellow in Fall
Green's Law: Anything's possible if you don't know what you're talking about.
Gresham's Law: [Thomas Gresham] Bad behavior tends to replace good.
groan-up: [grown-up mondegreen] adult so old that they groan when getting up
grobian: [Brandt's St. Grobianus] satiristically boorish and uncooth
grorange: [blue : grue :: orange : ?] green, of a leaf which will be turning orange in Fall
grossty: [J. Michael Straczynski] ten gross, 1,440
grown: [blue : grue :: brown : ?] green, of a leaf which will be turning brown in Fall
grubble: [paleologism] grope
grueberry: [blue : grue :: blueberry : ?, with from grue (Nelson Goodman, 1946)] still green, unripe blueberry, which will turn blue
grusome: [GRU (generalized repunit) back-formation] with repeated digit string
gry words: [Bob Grant] angry, hungry, meagry, but arguably also aggry [kind of African glass bead], cliffhangry, doppelgangry, forgry, gunslingry, humdingry, iggry [Arabic "hurry up"], imagry, malingry, maugry [var. of "maugre"], messagry, passengry, puggry [pith helmet scarf], scavengry, superangry, superhungry, teenagry, unangry, unhungry, wagry, warmongry
Gualtieri's Law: "Where there's a will, there's a won't."
guessation: [guess + gestation portmanteau] process of coming up with an answer that one almost remembers
guesstimation: [guess + estimation portmanteau] includes error maximizing, optimizing and minimizing varieties
guestbook: [mondegreen] book borrowed by or left behind by a guest
Gummidge's Law: "'Expertise' varies inversely with common knowledge."
gunk ho: [gung ho mondegreen] exclamation from the lookout upon sighting a gunk hole
gussy: [Gus + -y compound] Augustine-like
gutteral: g, k, kh
gyeong: [Sino-Korean] ten-to-the-sixteenth, sixteenplex, 10^{16}
gyrbwym: [acronym] "Gather ye rose buds while ye may."
gyromaniac: [gyroscope + pyromaniac portmanteau] person who insanely runs around after setting him/herself on fire rather than falling and rolling on the ground
gwawdodyns: [Welsh] 9 + 2 + 10 + 9 = 30-syllable quatrain rhyming aaba with internal rhyme of b in b or last verse
gwenders: [paleologism] cold tingling feeling
Gwetrustod: ["in God we trust" wordle] once and future motto of US
gwho: [A. B. Johnson] word used to conceal the absurdity of the unobservable, "subconscious", "quarks", "tachyon"
h-buccalized: describes word whose h changed to a th phoneme: hair (there), hat (that), hatch (thatch), he (Thee), hem (them), hey (they), ho (though)
H-graphable: [hexagon, Leonard Gordon] word graphable on hexagonal tiling– magnetohydrodynamically
h-invariant: word with h in 8th place: actorish, admonish, aerolith, airbrush, airworthy, algorithm, although, altogether, amaranth, apocrypha, approach, astonish, avalanche, ...
ha'ir: [split hair charade wordle] ultrafine point
habla: [Mayan] twenty-to-the-seventh, one-billion-two-hundred-eighty-million, 20^7 = 1,280,000,000
had-been: [has-been back-formation] former failure who has made a come-back
hae: [Sino-Korean] ten-to-the-twentieth, twentyplex, 10^{20}

haecceity: that which makes something or someone different from anything or anyone else

Hagari: describes words which change to another word when a double vowel with an h between is reduced to the vowel: graham (gram), nihil (nil), nohow (now), see Af Jinni

haikai: [Jap.] number or poem with 5 + 7 + 5 + 2(7) = 31 syllables

haiku: [Jap.] number or mood setting poem, usually with seasonal reference with 5 + 7 + 5 = 17 syllables

haikization: ["Potential Literature" by Queneau] erasing all of a poem except the rhyming sequences: "Lamb, lamb, lamb, lamb, snow, went, went, went, went, go" like reverse bouts-rimés

hair trigger: [mondegreen] pet hair that triggers allergic reaction

Haldane's Law: [J. B. S. Haldane] The universe's not only queerer than we imagine, it's queerer than anyone CAN imagine.

half-galleon: [half-gallon + galleon portmanteau] large volume measure, equare to two quarterdecks

half-right: both half-left and half-wrong at the same time, see strike-out

halferdasher: [haberdasher malapropism] athlete who runs a half-marathon

halfrhyme: rhyme of final consonant but not final vowel sound

halfway: [Christopher McManus] describe word equidistant from two shiftgrams: jig (age, ski with 1, 7, 5 shifts), wig (age, ski with 27, 33, 31 shifts), wit (age, ski with 53, 59, 57 shifts), googol (fusile, hikers), repent (octavo, uglify), smooch (pulped, vernal)

halluci-nation: [hallucination hyphenym] folie á deux that has spread throughout a whole country

hamartia: error of judgement

Hamming distance: counts difference between two numbers' binary expression

handkerchief: kerchief arbitrarily limited to use only to hands

handsom: [handsone + hansom portmanteau] good-looking, horse-drawn carriage

hanghasa: [Sino-Korean] ten-to-the-fifty-second, fifty-twoplex, 10^{52}

haneedleystack: [needle in haystack wordle] something found with extreme difficulty

hangle: [hanger + tangle portmanteau] cluster of coat hangers

Hanlon's Razor: "Never attribute to malice, if stupidity serves.", see Ulmann's Razor

haplograph: copyist error in which text is deleted because of identity of initial and final element: "To be or not is the question."

happen-stance: [happenstance hyphenym] hero/ine pose just before going into action when something calling for heroics happens

Harden's Law: "Whenever you have a terrific idea, someone else thought of it first."

Hardin's Law: [Garrett Hardin] You can't ever do only one thing.

hardship: [mondegreen] model ship not made of paper or balsa wood

Harris's Law: [Sidney J. Harris] Any philosophy that can be put "in a nutshell" belongs there.

haverlog: [haverlogarithm] logarithm of square root of ten times a number, $\log\sqrt{10}n$

Hawaska: [Hawaii + Alaska portmanteau] archipelago in the Pacific containing states of Hawaii and a shrunken Alaska

head effect: initial digit(s) are more memorable than any other number characteristic

heaholed: [hole in head wordle] touch of insanity

heamarriagemadeven: [marriage made in heaven wordle] hierogamy

heartfelt: thin, soft, red, fuzzy material for cutting out valentines

heatwave: [mondegreen] wave of a hand-held fan to provide cooling on a hot day

heavyweight: referring to a number with weight per length greater than 6

heavenscent: [heaven-sent mondegreen] incense-like odor
héblo: [D'ni] twenty-five-to-the-twentith, not-so-little twentyplex, 5^{40}
hedgehog: [mondegreen] person who tends to monopolize side bets
height: super-logarithm of the tenth super-root, number of tetrations in a number's equivalent of stacked tens' power tower
Hein's Law: [Piet Hein] "Problems worthy of attack prove their worth by hitting back."
Heinz: [Bingo] fifty-seven, 57
help-your-selfish: selfish went helping oneself
hendiadys: figure of speech substituting two nouns and conjunction for adjective and noun
hent: seize, carry away, experience or reach
hereoglyph: [here + hieroglyph portmanteau] little stick figure and/or arrow on "You Are Here" sign
herepin: [here + pin portmanteau ≈ hairpin] pin down a runaway piece of paper or currency with one's foot before the wind blows it out of reach
heretoofore: [heretofore mondegreen] long before here-and-now
Herman: Tom Swiftie-like sentence that ends with a proper name rather than an adverb: "She's my woman," said Herman. "I'm drawn to you," said Art. "Testing, testing," said Mike. "Pass me the binoculars," said Seymore.
Hermanette: Tom Swiftie-like sentence that end with overlapping quote and proper name rather than an adverb: "It's a jungle!" Jim said. ""Hickory, dickory," Doc said. "How do you like your eggs," Benedict asked. "Your welcome," Matt replied.
Hermione: Tom Swiftie-like sentence that end with overlapping proper name rather than an adverb: "You're a saint," Peter exclaimed. "What's for supper, mother?" Teresa asked.
herocksad: [rocks in head wordle] crazy ideas
Herrnstein's Law: [Richard Herrnstein] Total attention paid to an instructor's constant regardless of class size.
hesnowballck: [snow ball in heck wordle] very slim kind of chance
hesternopothia: yearning for the "Good Old Days", nostalgia
heterarchy: [hetero- + -archy compound] hierarchy that turns back on itself to form loops
heterocline: irregular, unorthodox, abnormal, deviating from the common, having haecceity
heteroliteral: passage in which each word shares no letters with its neighbors: "On a midnight, cool and foggy, as I pondered, light and groggy, ancient books and musty ledgers, not remembered anymore ..."(Eric Albert)
heterological: [Grelling's paradox] not self-describing: "heterological" or Berry's number, "This sentence contains four words.", "This sentence contains thirty-five letters.", "This sentence is in French."
heteronimble: [heteronym + nimble portmanteau] series of heteronymous puns
heterony: describes words which would be heteronyms if a final letter were added: tea
heteronym: word with same spelling but different pronunciation and meaning: axes, bass, content, drawer, entrance, incense, minute, moped, palsy, tear, toots
heteronymn: word that would be a heteronym if the final letter were deleted: teary
heterosectional: [heterosexual + sectional portmanteau] describing a love seat with separate places for the man and woman
hetuhila: [Sanskrit] ten-to-the-thirty-third, thirty-threeplex, 10^{33}
hetvindriya: [Sanskrit] ten-to-the-thirty-seventh, thirty-sevenplex, 10^{37}
hexagon: [hex a-gone mondegreen] curse-removing geometrical shape

hfitmhoap: [Isabella S. Stephenson acronym] "Holy Father, in Thy mercy, hear our anxious prayer."

hiddenym: [hidden + -nym] word hidden between the end of one word and the beginning of the next word: thee, do, new, Dan, go, hen, two

hideaway: with number name hidden away in longer number name, such as THREE in two hundred one

Higgledy-Piggledy: [Anthony Hecht] with first and fifth lines double dactyls and second the subject, rhyming abcdefgd

hihotr: [Washington acronym] "Heaven itself has ordained the right."

hiifwo: [Froude acronym] "Human improvement is from within outward."

hil: ["hinc illae lacrimae" acronym] therefore these tears

Hildebrand's Law: The quality of a department is inversely proportional to the number of courses listed in its catalog.

hílen: [D'ni] twenty-five-to-the-eighteenth, not-so-little thirty-sixplex, 5^{36} = 14,551,915,228,366,851,806,640,625

hímel: [D'ni] twenty-five-to-the-nineteenth, not-so-little thirty-eightplex, 5^{38} = 363,797,880,709,171,295,166,015,625

hindsite: [hindsight mondegreen] what one sees in a rear view mirror

hippomonstroziticorumbatous: [hippomonstrosesquipedalian + zitcorumbatous portmanteau] describes a 27-letter nonce word

hippopotomonstrosesquipedalian: [monstrous hippo with six legs] pertaining to word as long as hippopotomonstrosesquipedalian (30 letters)

híra: [D'ni] twenty-five-to-the-sixteenth, not-so-little thirty-twoplex, 5^{32} = 23,283,064,365,386,962,890,625

Hiram's Law: Consult enough experts and you can confirm anything, (but too many experts disconfirm it.)

hirer-ups: [higher-up mondegreen] employer's employers

hîs: [D'ni] twenty-five-to-the-seventeenth, not-so-little thirty-fourthplex, 5^{34} = 582,076,609,134,674,072,265,625

hitcov: [Aesop acronym] "Hypocrisy is the cloak of villainy."

hithoth: [Douglas Jerrold acronym] "Humor is the harmony of the heart."

hitrov: [Cicero acronym] "Honor is the reward of virtue.", see torovis

hiwthi: [acronym] "Home is where the heart is."

hliht: [Grover Cleveland acronym] "Honor lies in honest toil."

ho'oponopono: [Hawaiian] solving a problem by talking it out in something like a combination of locked-door arbitration and religious ceremony

hoacele: [ace in the hole wordle] unsuspected resources

hobson-jobson: corruption of foreign word or phrase to resemble more familiar one: acorn (akern), belfry (berfrey), compound (kampong),curry favor (Favel), forlorn (verloren), helpmate (helpmeet), hangnail (angenaegl), penthouse (apentis), pickaxe (picois), reindeer (hreinn), saltcellar (saltsaler), shamefaced (sceamfaest)

hoe hum: [hohum mondegreen] sound made by vibrating hoe

Hofstadter's Law: [Douglas Hofstadter] It always takes longer than you expect, even when you take into account Hofstadter's Law.

holey: describing number with digits with holes, 0, 4, 6, 8 or 9

holorhyme: whole-line rhyme: Victor Hugo's "O! Fragéles Hebreux! Allez, Rébecca, tombe! Offre ... Gilles zèbres, oeufs; ... l'Erèbeén, catombe."

home groan: [home grown mondegreen] expression expressed at home rather than at work

homi: ["Haec olim meminisse ivvabit." acronym] Time heals all things.

hommonym: [homonym + -m-] word which becomes its own homonym when an interior letter is deleted: aunt, bhang, boarder, boulder, burrow, gauge, hoarse, mooed, reign, too, two, whale

homnym: [homonym contraction] word which becomes its own homonym when an interior letter is added: ant, bang, bolder, border, gage, horse, mood, rein, to

homoantonym: words which are homonyms of antonyms: knights (nights), daze (days)

homocharade: [homonym + charade portmanteau] phrase pronounced like a word: a basement (abasement), a board (aboard), can sell (cancel), can't elope (cantaloupe), I deal, (ideal), knocked urn (nocturne)

homoconsonantic: describes preserving sequence of consonants but not the vowel: At a bier, a nutty boy, too, heats the queasy tone. (To be or not to be that is the question.)

homoeuteleuton: repetition of final phoneme, rhyming homograph

homoliteral: passage in which each word shares at least one letter with its neighbors: "On one midnight, cold and dreary, while I, faintly, weak and weary, pondered many a quaint and ancient volume of forgotten lore ..." (Eric Albert); passage in which words share initial letter(s) with predecessor's final and final(s) with its successor's initial: "Shimmering, gleaming, glistening, glow: winter reigns, splendiferous snow!" (Mary J. Hazard); chain contracted to continuous letter sequence: above example becomes: "shimmeringleaminglisteninglowintereignsplendiferousnow"

homolexical: aka vocabularycleptic, describes preserving a sentence's words but not their order: "To be that is not the question to be or ..."

homological: self-describing: "homological", "This sentence contains five words.", "This sentence is in English.", "This sentence contains thirty-six letters.", "In this sentence there are sixteen words, eighty-one letters, one hyphen, four commas, and one period."

homonimble: [homonym + nimble portmanteau] series of homonymous puns: "You think your poet's witty? I know poet that's Whittier. He's not so great; I've a cheese grater." "Malo malo malo malo." ("I'd rather be in an apple tree Than an evil man in adversity.");

homonum: [homonym back-formation] number that sounds the same as another number as in numbers read in different bases

homony: [curtailed homonym, hominy mondegreen] describing words which become their own homonym when a final, silent letter is added: ad, be, bell, bloc, born, but, by, canvas, cast, dam, flu, for, in, laps, main, or, pleas, so, teas, to, wet; wine; wind; wither; wet; wine

homonym: [Lat.] aka homophone, word that sounds the same but with a different meaning and spelling: air, e'er, ere, heir; all, awl; allowed, aloud; ascent, assent; ate, eight; aural, oral; ball, bawl; bare, bear; based, baste; better, bettor; bole, boll, bowl; borough, bough, bow; brake, break; canon, cannon; carat, caret, carrot; cast, caste; cereal, serial; chased, caste; choir, quire; coal, kohl; colonel, kernel; core, corps; council, counsel; cymbal, symbol; dew, do; doe, dough; ewe, you; fain, fane, feign; faint, feint; faun, fawn; feel, fee'll; feat, feet; flair, flare; flea, flee; foul, fowl; gamble, gambol; grate, great; hear, here; heed, he'd; heel, he'll; hew, hue, Hugh; hoes, hose; idle, idyll, idol; in gray she ate, ingratiate; incite, insight; knead, kneed, need; kneel, knee'll; know, no; main, mane, Maine; marshall, martial; meat, meet, mete; metal, mettle; missal, missile; missed, mist; moan, mown; nay, neigh; paced, paste; pail, pale; pause, paws; peak, peek, pique; pedal, peddle; peer, pier; pervade, purveyed; place, plaice; plum, plumb; pole, poll; pores, pours; praise, prays, preys; quarts, quartz; rain, reign, rein; raise, rays, raze; rapped, rapt, wrapped; read, red; read, reed; real, reel; reck, wreck; right, rite, write; rye, wry; sail, sale; scintillate, sin till late; sew, so, sow; sign, sine; sole, soul; son, sun; stair, stare; stationary, stationery; steal, steel; suede, swayed; suite, sweet; tail, tale; tare, tear; teal, tea'll; team, teem; there, their, they're; thyme, time; to, too, two; vain, vane, vein; vary, very; whales, wails; wain, wane; watt, what; way, weigh, whey; weak, week; weal, we'll, wheel; weed, we'd; you'll, Yule

homonymn: [homonym + -n] word which becomes its own homonym when a silent final letter is deleted: add, bee, belle, block, borne, butt, bye, canvass, caste, damn, flue, fore, inn, lapse, ore, please, sow, too, wee, whale, whet, whine, whined, wined, whither

homovocalic: describes preserving sequence of vowels but not the consonants: Lode of gold ore affirms evening's crown. (To be or not to be that is the question.)

hood wink: [hoodwink charade] brief closing of one eye to signal a criminal accomplice, see crime wave

hope: [Pierre Simon de LaPlace] sum of probabilities times their relative benefits for a given return

Hormesis paradox: Exposure to small doses of toxins can have beneficial effects.

hors dervish: [hors d'oeuvre + dervish] waiter/ess moving too quickly for the guests to snatch appetizers

hospitable: [David Silverman] word which forms addanyms for every addable position: cares, scares, cadres, caries, carets, caress

hot-headed: [hotheaded hyphenym] describing a word beginning with hot- but not referring to hot: hotchpot, hotel, hotelier

hotch: [paleologism] wiggle; swarm

household: [mondegreen] hold on a house for sale to a potential buyer

hózh'q: [Navaho] beauty that is not only in the eye but from the heart of the beholder and spreading out into the rest of creation

hsüeh: [Chinese] knowledge available to anyone willing to study

htowal: [Schiller acronym] "He that's overcautious will accomplish little."

hudibrastic: [*Hudibras* by Samuel Butler] humorous poem with 2(8) = 16 syllables rhyming a^2

huitain: [Fren.] poem with 6(8) = 48 syllables rhyming $abab^2cbc$ or ab^2a^2cac

humding: [humdinger back-formation] what a bell ringer who accompanies him/herself on a kazoo does

humoronimble: [cumulonimbus cloud + humorous + nimble portmanteau] refers to clown that's both humorous and nimble

hunter-gatherer: [mondegreen] owner of hunting lodge

hurkle: [paleologism] draw up limbs especially from pain

hushion: footless sock or useless creature

huxt: [huckster back-formation] sell to a reluctant huxtee with high-pressure techniques

Huxley's Effect: false thinking eventually produces wrong conduct

hwyl: [Welsh] emotional or eloquent outburst

hydration: adding a letter at the beginning of a word

hybread: [hybed + bread portmanteau] multi-grain bread

hydrocondiment: [hydro- + condiment] watery discharge that accumulates in the mustard or ketchup bottle that comes out first

hyp-henym: word transformed into another by having a hyphen added: coop, recover, recreate, see hyphenym

hyphenym: [hyphen + -nym portmanteau] word transformed into another by having hyphen deleted, see hyp-henym

hyper-mega-astronomical: [Scott Aaronson] $^49 \approx {}^410$
hypercomparative: [super : hyper :: superlative : ?] describes misapplying comparative suffix, -er, and/or superlative suffix, -est: better, betterer, betterest; best, bester, bestest; ever, everer, everest
hypernumber: [Neil Kelvie] indeterminate number like i-to-the-ith, that has infinitely many possible values
hypmosis: [hypnosis + osmosis portmantueau] extracting memories via hypnotic regression
hypnocratic: [hypnotic + Hippocratic] governing of the unaware by suggestion
hysteron-proteron: cart-before-the-horse word reversal
i-invariant: word with i in 9th place: accusatrix, achromatic, acrophobia, aeronautic, aerophobia, allergenic, allotropic, alphabetic, amanuensis, androgenic, anesthesia, ...
I-keili: describes words with only i as a vowel: I'm, in, is, it, prim, primitivistic
I-so-late: [isolate mondegreen] please don't shun me because of my tardiness
iagoats: [Victor Hugo acronym] "Inspiration and genius -- one and the same."
iamwimf: [Shakespeare acronym] "I am wealthy in my friends."
iatronym: [Virginia R. Hager's doctored name] word beginning with dr- that generates a fictitious name: Dr. Acula, Dr. Eamer, Dr. Inker
ibebious: ["I believe everyone believes it." acronym back-formation] believing that all others believe
ibibious: ["I believe I believe it." acronym acronym back-formation] believing that you believe
ibidbious: ["I believe I don't believe it." acronym back-formation] believing that you disbelieve
ibidinous: [libidinous beheading] with many references from one source
ibidious: ["I believe I disbelieve it." acronym back-formation] believing that you disbelieve
ibious: ["I believe it!" acronym back-formation] believing, especially enthusiastically
ibohphobia: [beheaded aibohphobia] fear of alindromes
ibubious: ["I b(elieve yo)u b(elieve) i(t.)" grammanym back-formation] believing that another believes
ibudbious: ["I b(elieve yo)u d(on't) b(elieve) i(t.)" grammanym back-formation] believing that another disbelieves
icdeth: [Phil 4:13 acronym] "I can do everything through Him."
ickyology: [icky + ichthyology] study of icky things, goo, goop, slop, slime
idbabious: ["I don't believe anyone believes it." acronym back-formation] disbelieving that other believe
idbebious: ["I don't believe everyone believes it." acronym back-formation] disbelieving all others believe
idbibious: ["I don't believe I believe it." acronym back-formation] disbelieving that you believe
idbubious: ["I d(on't) b(elieve yo)u b(elieve) i(t.)" grammanym back-formation] disbelieving that another believes
idgi: ["I don't get it?" acronym] Huh?
idnea: ["In dubiis non est agendum." acronym] When in doubt, don't.
iede: ["Interfice errorem, diligere errantum." acronym] Hate the sin, love the sinner.
ieqha: [Ita erat quando hic adventi." acronym] It was that way when I got here.
ifbe: ["Ira furor brevis est." acronym] Anger's a brief insanity.
iff: [contraction] if and only if
iform: [uniform back-formation] different from all the others
ignight: [ignite mondegreen] light up the fireplace after sundown

ignortion: [ignore + ignition portmanteau] act of trying to start a car having forgotten that the engine is already started

ignore ant: [ignorant mondegreen] totally disregard insect pest

ignoratio elenchi: fallacy of "missing the point"

ihhp: [phhi ananym] ciscendental enverted from phi: ...001,643,338

ihp: [phi ananym] ciscendental enverted from phi: ...889,330,816.1

ijrikilijri: [ABCD : IJKL :: abracadabra : ?] nonsense word like abracadabra

ilc: [1LC grammanym] first-level consciousness

ilne: ["ignorantia legis nom excusat" acronym] ignorance of the law is no excuse

illth: [wealth back-formation] poverty

illywacker: [paleologism] trickster

Ikswopank's number: [Knapowski ananym] reverse of to-the-fifth-e-to-the-thirty-fifth rounded, R[$^5e^{35}$]

Iles's Law: [Greg Iles] "There is an easier way to do it."

imbo: [paleologism, imbecile contraction] simpleton, dupe

imfhamm: [acronym] "Lift up for yourself treasures in Heaven."

imp-polite: [impolite hyphenym] as courteous and thoughtful as an imp, that is, not at all

important: [Gresham] never to be resolved

impossible: [Norman Kagan] technically impossible (the undoable, I1K), scientifically impossible (the unthinkable, I2K), logically impossible (illogical by human perceptions, I3K) and

meaningless (beyond even new ways of doing, thinking or perceiving, I4K)

imposstor: [impostor + possum portmanteau] someone who plays dead like a possum

impromptwo: [impromptu mondegreen] spur-of-the-moment duet

impure: describes word with letters from both halves of the alphabet, front/back, inside/outside

imti: [In medio tutissimus ibis., "In the middle of things you will go most safe." acronym] moderation

in-crease: [increase hyphenym] fold a piece of paper toward one's self rather than away as opposed to folding away from one's self

in-formation: [information hyphenym] how an army marches

in-Seine: [insane mondegreen] describes person found dead in Parisian river

in-tents: [intence hyphenym] where circus performers perform

in-quest: [inquest hyphenym] search to find one's inner self

in-vest: [invest hyphenym] wearing a three-piece suit like a banker or stockbroker

inamania: [beheaded ainamania] abnormal desire for beheaded palindromes

inary: [2 : binary :: i : ?] referring to number based on i, including the improper kinds with A = 10, B = 11, C = 12, etc., Z = 35, j = 2i, k = 3i, etc., z = 18i, etc.

incide: [inside homonym] describes wordplay on -side/-cide suffixes: chop sueycide, flipcide, offcide

Incornish: [inkhornish mondegreen] academese with much Greek and Latin

indicake: [indicate + cake portmanteau] point out what one wants at the bakery without actually saying which one

indenumerable: transfinite number beyond the denumerables, such as aleph-aleph,$\aleph_\aleph$, to-the-infinite-infinity, $^\infty\infty$

ineqtdaa: [Syrus acronym] "It's not every question that deserves an answer."

infinite palindrome: "Never, ever, ever, ..., ever even!"; "Trap miss; I kiss; I kiss; ... , impart."

inflation: [Victor Borge] substitution of numerical homonyms of n by n +1: anytwo, atelevendant, awnine, classeven, estnine, fiveget, fivemer, fivethright, fivever, hnine, misbegoteleven, opporthreenity, saturten, sthreedent, twoce, threetor

infoo: mixture of information and misinformation, especially that which starts out reliable and turns not

informaldehyde: [informal + formaldehyde portmanteau] generic embalming fluid

information: [*Surely You're Joking, Mr. Feynman*] same in all representations though represented by few or many bits: 1/243 as power, 3^{-5} or repeating decimal, 0.00411522633774485559670781893

ingram: word formed from another by addition of a letter interiorly (epenthesis): a(g)round, (a)mess, (b)lame, b(l)ank, (b)ra(i)n,(b)ramble, bran(d), ch(i)ef, cla(i)m, clas(p)s, cor(o)net, den(o)ted, e(r)ase, (f)a(c)t, fa(r,c)e, go(a)d, (h)eater, h(e)aven, pa(n)ts, re(a)d, s(c)andal, (s,h)ave, s(m)ack, s(t)ew, (t)heater, (t,h)ick,(t,h)is, (t)on(e), t(h)rust, w(e)ary, w(h)en

inkhornish: [paleologism] ostentatiously learned, pendantic

innerword: [inword extrapolation] pure word with letters from the inner third of the alphabet (counting from blank as zero), a-to-h: ah, ah-ha, ace, age, cage, ha, ha-ha

innestword: [innerword extrapolation] pure word with letters from the more inner than the inner letters of the alphabet, a-to-e: ace, cee, deeded

inntact: [inn + intact portmanteau] consideration when dealing with fellow boarders

innumeracy: [John Allen Paulos] inability or unwillingness to understand basic math

inoe: ["Impossibilium nulla obligatio est." acronym] You don't have to do the impossible.

inrageous: [outrgeous antonym] normal, sedate

insertion-deletion network: [insertion-deletion] words linked by insertions or deletions, with maximum path between called "distance" and minimum "span": chatter, hatter, hater, heater, heather, …

insec: [curtailed "insect", AU : parsec :: inch : ?] 3.255442 mi = 5.239127 km

insomniactor: [insomniac + actor portmanteau] person pretending to sleepwalk

insteadfast: [instead + steadfast portmanteau] letting George remain faithful

insufficient fun: [doubly-curtailed insufficient funds] recreation that doesn't quite meet expectations

intaxification: [tax + intoxification portmanteau] euphoria at getting a tax refund, which lasts until realizing it was always your funds

interesting: [Edwin F. Bechenbach] true of every positive integer or [Nathaniel Johnston] integer not yet in *On-Line Encyclopedia of Integral Sequences*

interlox: [interlocks] word able to be broken up into two or more other words (interlocks): firebugs = fig + rebus

intotficse: [Einstein acronym] "I never think of the future; it comes soon enough."

intravention: [intervention back-formation] self-help in countering addiction

inuidlioc: ["in necessariis unitas, in dubis libertas, in omnibus caritas" acronym] in the necessary unity, in the doubtful liberty, in all charity

invariented: word with invariant(s), letter(s) in same position as in alphabet: acquaintanceship, agammaglobulinemias, antianthropomorphist, archership, back, band, ebb, counterobjection, hierarchical, interchangeableness, nondefensibleness, noninterventionalist, parallelogram, personality, quarterback, relief, resting, retrench, write

inword: [inward mondegreen] pure word with letters from the inner half of of the alphabet, a-to-m: hammamelidacae

iottco: [acronym] intuitively obvious to the casual observer

iottpate: [Aesop acronym] "It's one thing to propose, another to execute."
ip: [pi ananym] ciscendental enverted from pi, i. e., etc. ...356295141.3
iplibs: [Catherine II acronym] "I praise loudly; I blame softly."
Ipsit dixit: fallacy of arguing from dogmatic statement
irrational: [Jacques Bens] describe poem patterned after irrational number, π, 3 + 1 + 4 + 1 + 5 = 14-line sonnet
irreversible: compound words or phrases that change means when reversed– bypass, inlet, instill, outlay, outride, outtalk, overall, overcome, overdone, overstep, overturn, undergo, understand, understudy, underwrite, withhold
ishish: [-ish + -ish compond] not-so much like
isists: [Talmud acronym] "Iron sharpens iron; scholar, the scholar."
isogram: [Dmitri Borgmann] aka heterogram (Susan Thorp), "disogram" (Ted Clarke), haplogram (J. H. Marshall), word with no letters repeated: adventurously, ambidextrously, bracketing, constipated, dermatoglyphics, documentary, dumbwaiter, endolymphaticus, facetiously, postneuralgic, questionably, slotmachine, stenographic, subordinately, sympathizer, uncopyrightables, valedictory, workmanship, zymogenics
isolano: word not transformable into any other word by addition or deletion: cwm, ebb, emu, gnu, gyp, imp, ism, its, nth, obi, ohm, ova, urn, use
isomorph: word or number which has the same sequential pattern as another: barbarian = 123123425 = murmurous
isomorphology: sequential pattern of a word or number: pi (12324564314...)
isopangram: sentence using all 26 letters just once: "Cwm fjord-bank glyphs vex quiz.", "Nth black fjord vex Qum gyp wiz.", "Benjy G. 'Quit' Schwartzkopf, LXV, M. D."
isosceles: word able to be transdeleted into smaller and smaller words down to a single letter, see rhope: befriends, definers, refined, finder, diner, rind, din, in, I; crotchets, crochet, torches, throes, short, shot, hot, to, O; desperate, repeated, tapered, parted, trade, tear, rat, at, a; destruction, introduces, reduction, doctrine, cordite, direct, tired, diet, tie, it, I; drafting, trading, rating, train, rant, tan, at, a; filament, inflame, menial, limen, limn, nim, in, I; flattering, faltering, integral, granite, rating, train, rain, ran, an, a; flirters, trifles, strife, first, rift, fir, if, I; inventors, investor, ventors, strove, trove, over, ore, or, O; myriads, dismay, maids, said, aid, id, I; reactivation, ratiocinate, recitation, intricate, interact, nitrate, attire, irate, rate, art, at, a; representational, transperitoneal, presentational, septentrional, steprelational, interseptal, eternalist, reinstate, interest, entries, insert, reins, rise, sir, is, I; roasted, trades, darts, arts, rat, at, a; shortens, thrones, hornet, thorn, torn, nor, or, O; thinned, hinted, thine, thin, tin, in, I; thorniest, horniest, throne, honest, stone, tone, eon, no, O; transpires, restrains, strainer, retains, strain, train, rain, ran, an, a
isosyntaxism: maintainence of syntax while changing text's words
isotetragrammed: word with letter repeated four times in succession: Llanfairpwllgwynngyllgogerychwyrndrobwllllantysiliogogoch, Wales
isotrigrammed: word (or nonword) with letter repeated three times insuccession: abbessship, ballless, baronessship, bellless, billless, brrr, bullless, bzzz, bzzzbzzz, callless, cellless, chilless, chlorophyllless, Churchillless, countessship, dellless, dollless, drillless, duchessship, empressship, enchantressship, fallless, frillless, gallless, gillless, godessship, goodwillless, governessship, grillless, hallless, handbillless, headmistressship, heiressship, hellless, hillless, hmmm, hostessship [*The Winter's Tale* IV, iv],hullless, idyllless, jellless, knellless, krillless, mallless, millless, ogressship, patronessship, pffft, photocellless, pillless, prioressship, quillless, refillless, rillless, seductressship, shellless, sillless, skullless, smellless,

spellless, spillless, squallless, stallless, stillless, thrillless, trillless, wallless, waterfallless, willless, yellless

ispe: [ipsa scientia potestas est] knowledge is power

isocube: [isolated ice cube portmanteau] last icecube left by someone too lazy to refill the ice tray

itastmaw: [acronym] "It takes all sorts to mke a world."

itiltih: [acronym] "If there is life, there is hope."

itsfof: [Charles Caleb Colton acronym] "Imitation's the sincerest form of flattery."

itsy-bitsy: smaller than teeny-weeny (9 letters)

iuts: [Aesop acronym] "In unity there's strength."

iversal: [universal back-formation] referring to outside the universe, in God's mind

iykwim: [acronym] if you know what I mean

ja: [Sino-Korean] ten-to-the-twenty-fourth, twenty-fourplex, 10^{24}

jack-of-all-thumbs: [Jack-of-all-trades + all-thumbs portmanteau] inept fixer

Jacob's Law: To err's human, blaming it on someone else even more so.

jae: [Sino-Korean] ten-to-the-forty-fourth, forty-fourplex, 10^{44}

Jagari: describes words which change to another word when a double vowel with a j between is reduce to the vowel: dojo (do), rajah (rah), rejector (rector), see Af Jinni

jambory: [jamboree back-formation] ruled by uninhibited mobocracy

Javanese stuttering: repetition of syllables: "Poème pour bégue" by Jean Lescure, bananana, mamama, papapa, poohpoohpooh, so-so-so, ta-ta-ta, toot-toot-toot

jhonestun: [honest injun wordle] extremely honest

jic: [acronym] just in case

jiff: [jiffy back-formation] ample time for a task

jeezly: [paleologism] miserable, rotten, unfortunate, inferior, dull, ill-conceived

jeong: [Sino-Korean] ten-to-the-fortieth, fortyplex, 10^{40}

jink: [paleologism] quickly evade; swindle

jo: [Jap.] ten-to-the-twenty-fourth, twenty-fourplex, but also [Sino-Korean] ten-to-the-twelfth, twelveplex, 10^{12}

joac: ["Justitia omni auro carior" acronym] justice is more precious than gold

jockular: [jock + jocular portmanteau] not taking athletics seriously

joeys: words hidden within larger roonym, related in meaning to the larger, but not etymologically: amble (permabulate), bar (barricade), can (container), cocoa (chocolate), cue (clue), dead (deceased), is (exist), face (facade), last (latest), lie (recline), lies (calumnies), lit (illuminate), male (masculine), mart (market), mates (matches), partly (partially), pinned (pinioned), poses (postures), rage (rampage), rapscallion (rascal), rest (respite), ruin (destruction), rule (regulate), see (observe), sin (transgression), slid (slithered), sue (prosecute), tainted (contaminated), tombs (catacombs), tutor (instructor), unity (unanimity), urge (encourage), use (utilise), see roonym

jokelore: [joke + folklore portmanteau] humor so old that it has become anonymous and ubiquitous

jonnuk: [paleologism] honest, loyal, equitable, proper, customary, conclusive

jootsy: ["jumping out of the system" acronym + -y, Dzu Tse aka Jucius] referring to mathematics which can switch from Roman numerals to words to numbers at any time or literature in which a character can switch to the writer or reviewer (Van Veen in *Ada* or John Ray in foreword of *Lolita* both by Vladimir Nabokov)

jot: [acronym] Jesus, our Lord, see titl

jou: [Jap.] ten-to-the-twenty-eighth, twenty-eightplex, 10^{28}
Jourdain's paradox: double Epimenides paradox or Liar's paradox,
joyned: [join + joy portmanteau] feeling wedded bliss, in a happy, lasting marriage
joystick: [mondegreen] long-lasting euphoric feeling
jug-headed: [jugheaded hyphenym] describing a word beginning with jug- but not referring to jug: juggernaut, juggler, jugular
jump roach: [jump rope mondegreen] childhood game similar to leapfrog
Juneteenth: [June + -teenth compound] octave in mid-June between 13th and 19th
jungli: [paleologism ≈ jungley] uncouth, unrefined
juxta: [juxtaposition back-formation] very close like one's own shadow
K-graphable: [king's move, Leonard Gordon] word graphable as if by king's moves vertically, horizontally or diagonally: arterioplasties
k-invariant: describes words with k only in the 11th place: cabinetwork, cinderblock, countersink, cyberattack, diamondback, doublecheck, doublespeak, fiddlestick, leatherback, shuttlecock, sparrowhawk, steeplejack, weathercock
k-voiced: describes a word whose k phoneme turned to a g: cam (gam), cap (gap), cat (gat), coat (goat), cut (gut)
Kagari: describes words which change to another word when a double vowel with a k between is reduced to the vowel: biking (bing), diking (ding), piking (ping), see Af Jinni
kaisbouy: [Mt 7:7 acronym] "Knock and it shall be opened unto you."
kami-ku: [Japanese] 572-syllabled upper clause of waka
kan: [Jap.] ten-to-the-thirty-sixth, thirty-sixplex, 10^{36}, but [Mayan] four, 4
kankara: [Sanskrit] ten-to-the-thirteenth, thirteenplex, 10^{13}
karmageddon: [karma + armageddon portmanteau] bad karma overload
kathana: [Sanskrit] ten-to-the-one-hundred-twenty-sixth, hundred-twenty-sixplex, 10^{126}
kazillion: [Mayan ka- (20) + zillion] g(20, 3z + 3, 10)
keepsock: [keepsake + sock portmanteau] stocking that is kept year after year like thenone take out once a year at Christmastide
kei: [Jap.] ten-to-the-sixteenth, sixteenplex, 10^{16}
Kelly's Law: "Nothing's as simple as it seems."
kemp: [unkempt back-formation] immaculately maintain
kenning: [Anglo-Saxon] personal synonym
kerdumf: [paleologism] exclamation of surprise
kerfuffle: [paleologism] fuss, to-do
kernel: [col- mondegreen] describes word beginning with col- generating a fictitious name, Col. Lar, Col. Lum, Col. Lynn, Col. Ossus, Col. Umbus
keypunch: describes telephonym which uses each telephone number just once
khaloss: [paleologism] exhausted, finished, dead
kharva: [Sanskrit] ten-to-the-forty-second, forty-twoplex, 10^{42}
kidnapkining: [kidnap + napkin portmanteau] taking unused napkins from restaurant
kilillion [kilo- + -illion] ten-to-the-three-thousand-third, three-thousand-threeplex, $10^{3,003}$
killion: [Ian Frazer] number so huge it can cause brainnumbing or brainlock, not to be confused with mere killillion
kindread: [kindred mondegreen] irrational fear of one's own family
kinatic: [kinetic + fanatic portmanteau] describing a person obsessive about exercise
kip: [acronym] "Knowledge is power."
Kitman's Law: [TV critic Marvin Kitman] Pure drivel drives out ordinary drivel.

kitschen: [kitsch + kitchen portmanteau] sentimental, not-so high quality cook's room

knaive: [knave + naive portmanteau] describes scoundrel wannabe

Knapowski's number: [Stanisław Knapowski] to-the-fifth-e-to-the-thirty-fifth

Knight's Law: Life is what happens to you while you are making other plans.

knighted: [Sir/ser-, sir-, sur- mondegreen] describes word beginning with cir-/ser-/sir-/sur- that generates a fictitious name, Sir Bian, Sir Cumference, Sir Fer, Sir Geon, Sir Loin, Sir Mon, Sir Occo, Sir Pentine, Sir Prize, Sir Rum, Sir Upy, Sir Veyor, Sir Vivor

knock knock: pun in the form of: "Knock Knock!", "Who's there?", "– who?": "Abigail 's blowing in.", "Adolph in swimming by","Anna gonna tell you.", "Boo who? Don't cry!', "Dolores be an England","Mary Christmas", "Yolanda big fish with the right bait"

Kolbe: [Maximillian Kolbe] St. Maximillian's number given by Nazis, 16,670

koogol: [Matt Hudelson] kduplex, ten-to-the-tenth-to-the-kth, $^210^k$

Konigsberg's Law: [Woody Allen Konigsberg] 80% of success is showing up.

Koppett's Law: The probability of an outcome with the greatest inconvenience for the largest number approaches 100%. (See Meyer's Law.)

kotippakoti: [Sanskrit] ten-to-the-twenty-first, twenty-oneplex, 10^{21}

kou: [Jap.] ten-to-the-thirty-second, thirty-twoplex, 10^{32}

kougasha: [Jap.] ten-to-the-fifty-second, fifty-twoplex, 10^{52}

koyaanisqatsi: [Hopi] life style so out of balance as to call for a new life style

Kranzberg's Laws : [Melvin Kranzberg] (1) Technology is neither good nor bad; nor is it neutral. (2) Invention is the mother of necessity. (3) Technology comes in packages, big and small. (4) Nontechnical factors take precedence in technology-policy decisions. (5) All history is relevant, but the history of technology is the most relevant. (6) Technology is a very human activity.

Kristol's Law: [William Kristol] "Being frustrated is disagreeable, but real disasters begin with getting what you want."

kshobhya: [Sanskrit] ten-to-the-seventeenth, seventeenplex, 10^{17}

kula: [Trobriand Islander] never-ending cycle of gift and gift history sharing

kumuda: [Sanskrit] ten-to-the-hundred-fifth, hundred-fiftyplex, 10^{150}

kyrielle: [Fren.] poem with 4n(7) syllables rhyming Aab^2Aac^2, where A is refrain

kyth: [Madeline L'engle] communicate like angels, see grok

kwuccpfol: [gifts of the Spirit acronym] knowledge, wisdom, understanding, council, courage, piety, fear of the lord

l-invariant: describing word with l only in the twelfth place: adventureful, antediluvial, aeronautical, anthropological, arithmetical, assymmetrical, bicentennial, catechetical, coincidental

la rien que la toute la: ["the nothing but everything the", François Le Lionnais] text without nouns, verbs or adjectives

lacing form: [racing form malapropism] manikin for practicing different ways to lace a corset

lacouith: [acronym] "Light a candle of understanding in thine heart."

Lagari: describes words which change to another word when a double vowel with an l between is reduced to the vowel: Alan (an), arm (alarm), as (alas), dryly (dry), gayly (gay), licit (lit), piling (ping), prolong (prong), scalar (scar), shyly (shy), stalag (stag), tiling (ting), wiling (wing), wryly (wry), see Af Jinni

lagniappe: [Creole] unexpected bonus or gratuity beyond the terms of a contract written or tacit, reward for patient or friendly potential customer

laighead: [Hugh Downs' lay + egghead portmanteau] non-professional, yet well-read science fan

lakh: [Indian] aka laksha, hundred thousand, 10^5

lall: [acronym] "Live and let live."

lallated: describes a word whose l is changed to a w: lack (wack), lag (wag), lake (wake), late (wait), lay (way), lend (wend), Lent (went), lo (woe)

lallih: [acronym] "Life's a long lesson in humility."

land mime: [land mine + mime portmanteau] mime that threatens to explosively break through the non-existent glass wall

Langin's Law: If things were left to chance, they'd be better.

laniciv: [vicinal ananym] word with no letters alphabetical neighbors: laniciv, vicinal, with, word

lapsus linguae: *O Novo Guia da Conversação en Portuguez e Inglez* by Jos,da Fonseca (1855): "Do you cut the hairs?" "Who are you beautiful." "Sit down us to the shade." "You hear the birds gurgling." see Franglais, Macaronic

larder: [lard back-formation] with more filler than the original text

larding: [Paul Fournel] variation of tireur a la ligne (line pulling), adding intercalation (labeled with letter) between original text's paragraphs (labeled by number) with new characters and plot angles

large: [Eliezer S. Yudkowsky] as high or higher than the thirty-second busy beaver number, whatever that may be

latinym: [Latin + -nym and la + ti + -nym] word formed from another by substituting so-fa syllables for alphabetical notes, i. e., a = la, b = ti, c = do, d = re, e = mi, f = fa, g = so: favor = flavor, grabs = gratis, mad = mare, see pianonym

laughing stock: [mondegreen] domesticated hyenas

lawn cheer: [lawn chair + cheer portmanteau] euphoria that your yard looks better than the Jones's

law firm: [mondegreen] precident unlikely to be overruled

leadwait: [leadweight mondegreen] subjectively long duration of a fatal bullet's traveling from barrel to victim

leapfrog: describes word formed from another by compounding even letters with odds or v. v.: feast = fat + es = fates, freer = fer + re = refer, heart = hat + er = hater, steal = ael + ta = tassel, see jump roach

leapian: someone born of February 29, Leap Day, with about one quarter of the birthdays of everyone else

Le Chatelier's Law: If some stress is brought to bear on a system in equilibrium, the equilibrium is displaced in the direction which tends to undo the effect of the stress.

legend-demain: [legerdemain hyphenym] process by which historical facts can "magically" become legendary

Legion's number of the first kind: to-the-second-six-hundred-sixty-six, $^2666 > 10^{1,880}$

Legion's number of the second kind: to-the-second-six-hundred-sixty-six-factorial, $^2666!$

Leibniz's Law: aka Identity of Indiscernibles, If two objects have all their properties in common, then they are one and the same object.

length: number of digits a number has, its rounded logarithm

Lescurian: iterative literature generation designation of the form $C_i + N_i + M_i$, C indicating syntactic category, N and M two numerical parameters: S + 7 = stepping seven substantives further along in a designated list

lettershift: [Dmitri Borgmann] shifting each letter of a word the same distance through the "round-the-horn" alphabet to another word: banjo (ferns), cheer (jolly), crib (lark), end (foe), fizz (knee), God (owl, sap, wet), ice (keg), odd (zoo), open (stir), pecan (tiger)
Leviathan: as high as or higher than six-hundred-sixty-six-factorialplex, $\geq 10^{666!}$
libadam: [Burns acronym] "Life is but a day at most."
lillih: [Barrie acronym] "Life is a long lesson in humility."
liaison: adding the ending of one word to the beginning of the following one, especially articles: admir(al), (a)pricot, (al)gebra, (al)ligator, (la)riat, a (n)adder, a (n)apron, a (n)ewt, a (n)umpire
lightwait: [lightweight mondegreen] practicing patience while the traffic light changes from rellow to yeen to green
lightweight: with weight per length less than 3
lif: ["lupus in fabula" acronym] the someone just talked about
likeness: aka Gleichniszahlen-Reihe and look-and-say with predecessor's digits counted out
liltais: [Holmes acronym] "Logic is logic, That's all I say."
limatherick: [mathematical + limerick] mathematical limerick: $12 + 144 + 20 + 3(\sqrt{4})/7 + 5(11) = 9^2 + 0_2$ ["A dozen, a gross and a score Plus three times the square root of four Divided by seven Plus five times eleven Is nine squared and not a bit more."]
limatherick chain: linked limericks in mathematical language: $y = 2\tan(\pi) + (4/6 + 1/3)(2(2z)/4 + e^{2\pi i}; 2!z = (2(20) - 20)(3,000,000^2)/(9 \times 10^{12}) + 343^{1/3}$ ["The unknown quantity, y, Equals twice the tangent of pi Plus four-sixths and a third Times twice two z quartered Plus e raised to double pi i", while "Two factorial z Equals two score less twenty Times the square of three million Divided by nine trillion Plus the cube root of three forty-three.", so z = 10 and y = 11]
limbaginary: [imaginary + limb portmanteau] describes phantom arm or leg
limber: [timber malapropism] exclamation by gymnastics coach to warn students lesson is beginning
limer: limerick with ending deleted, rhyming aabb
limeraiku: [limerick, haiku portmanteau] poem or number with 5 + 7 + 5 syllables rhyming aba
limerick: 5 anapestic verses with three accents in 1st, 2nd and 5th, 2 on 3rd and 4th, rhyming aabba: "God's plans made a hopeful beginning, 'Til Adam and Eve started sinning. We trust that the story Will end in God's glory Though it seems the other side's winning.", "Hickory, dickory, dock, The mouse ran up the clock. The clock struck one And down it run, Hickory, dickory, dock.", "I sat next to the duchess at tea; I twas just as I feared it would be: Her rumblings abdominal Were truly phenomenal And everyone thought it was me!", "There once was a lady named Bright, Who traveled much faster than light. She went out one day In a relative way And returned the previous night.", "There once was an eloquent preacher Called a hen a most elegant creature. The hen pleased at that Laid an egg in his hat And thus did the hen reward Beecher."
limick: limerick with middle deleted, rhyming aaba
lindrome: [beheaded alindrome] near-palindrome that lacks first two letters
linkade: word able to be broken into two other words sharing the linking letter aiding the linkade: foreign (for reign)
lipodeuterologue: work never using a word twice: 200-page *Never Again* by Doug Nufer
lipogram: text without given letter(s): (1) each letter in turn: *Iliad* translated by Nestor of Laranda; Homer's *Odyssey* translated byTrypiodorus, *De Aetatibus Mundi et Hominis* by Fabius Planiciades Fulgentius, *Aurora* by Pierre de Riga (Bible canto résumés in verse), (2)

one letter throughout: (sigma) *Ode to the Centaurs and Hymn to Demeter* by Lasus of Hermione, c. 525 B. C.; (r, s-) *Xenium* translated by Janus Caecilius Frey, 1616; (abc-) *Ottilie von Riesenstein* by Franz Rittler (unpublished); (a, i, o, u-) *Eve's Legend* by Henry Richard Vassal-Fox Holland, 3 pp., 1836; *La Disparition* by Georges Perec, 300 pp.; (e-) 50,000-word *Gadsby* by Ernest Vincent Wright, 1939; (s-) "Mary had a little lamb With fleece a pale white hue And everywhere that Mary went The lamb kept her in view; To academe he went with her, Illegal and quite rare; It made the children laugh and play To see a lamb in there." by A. Ross Eckler

liponym: text without given word, *Contes sans qui ni que* by Henri de Chenevières, loveless "About This" by Vladimir Mayakovsky

lipophoneme: text without given phoneme

liposyllable: text without given syllable

liquid: l, r

liquiddate: [liquidate mondegreen] just joining someone for a drink

lisad: [Sgs 8:6 acronym] "Love is strong as death."

lisped: describes a word whose s changed to a th phoneme: lisp (lithp), sank (thank), sigh (thigh), sing (thing), sink (think), sump (thump)

litfotl: [Rom 13:10 acronym] "Love is the fulfillment of the Law."

litgor: [Trench acronym] "Logic is the grammar of reason."

litmop: [acronym] "Leisure is the mother of philosophy."

litterature: [litter + literature portmanteau] writing not worth reading

little: [little googol, two-to-the-hundredth, back-formation] reduced by division by all factors not two, little dozen = 4, little gross = 16, little million = 64

Littleton's number: [Dudley E. Littlewood] to-the-second-forty-twoplex, $^2 10^{42}$

Littlewood's Law: [E. Littlewood] "Individuals can expect miracles to happen to them, at the rate of about one per month."

llap: [Vulcan acronym] "Live long and prosper."

locost: [low cost + locust portmanteau] inexpensive insectivore pet food

logical vaccuum: [A. K. Dewdney] where logic is missing, because of missing information or frame of reference

logomotion: [logo- + locomotion portmanteau] not-so free association moving from one word or phrase to another via word or teauword: father, father figure, figure out, outact, act one, one step, stepson, son; out, outback, backdrop, dropoff, offside, sideline, lineup, up; see namedropping

logoog: [Jeroen Visser, googol ananym] zero followed by a hundred ones, $(10^{100} - 1)/9$

logorhythm: [logorithm mondegreen] syllable count pattern in arthmopoems

long: [échelle longue back-formation] ten-to-the-rounded-four-thirds-logarithm, as in long googol or ten-to-the-hundred-thirty-third, 10^{133}

looped: ["Ploo", Peter Newby] anagram formed by making the final letter initial: "ploo" (Old English, plough), "oplo" and "oopl", rather than those formed by other transpositions, lopo, lpoo, olop, oolp, oopl, opol, polo, pool

lop-sided: [mondegreen] sharper side of the knife blade that does the lopping

lost-and-found: indeterminate state of Schrödiger's cat

love pentangle: [love triangle extrapolation] diabolically complex love-hate relationships between five people

low cuss: [locust mondegreen] curse quietly under one's breath

low profile: [mondegreen] with large chin and so a head with a below-average center of gravity

Lubin's Law: If another scientist thought your research was more important than his, he would drop what he is doing and do what you are doing.

ludod: [Burns acronym] "Let us do or die."

ludism: playfulness

luff: [paleologism] work for two

lufoeoj: [Heb 12:2] "Let us fix our eyes on Jesus."

lunch pale: [lunch pail mondegreen] symptom of a bad mid-day meal

Lusitania number: [*Titanic* : *Lusitania* :: titanic : ?] with two thousand digits, $\log(n) \geq 2{,}000$

luna tic: [lunatic mondegreen] parasitic insect from the moon

lüshi: [Chin.] poem or number with 6(5 or 7) syllables

lusionist: [illusionist back-formation] user of artistic techniques to create a state of true perception of actual nature, to lead aright, to cause to accept as true or valid what is true or valid

Lyon's Law: He who hesitates is last.

lisys: [Euripides acronym] "Life is short, yet sweet."

m-invariant: describes words which as m only in the 13th place: aboriginalism, anticommunism, antisocialism, antiterrorism, catechumanism, counterreform, ecumenicalism, ferrochromium.

mabwtebwot: [Charles Caleb Colton acronym] "Men are born with two eyes and one tongue."

macaronic: (English as pseudo-Latin) "Apud in is almi de si re, Mimistres I ne ver re qui re, Alo veri findit a gestis His miseri ne ver atrestis." ("A pudding is all my desire. My mistress I never require. A lover, I find it a jest is. His misery never at rest is."), "Civilifortibus es inero. Demes nobus es demes trux." (See, Willy, forty buses in a row. Dem is no buses; dem is trucks."), "Mollis abuti En qui tecuti; No lasso finis. Molli divinis." (Molly's a beauty and quite a cutie; No lass so fine is. Molly divine is.") "O mi de armis tres Iminadis tres Cantu disco ver Meas alo ver?" (O my dear mistress, I'm in a distress. Can't you discover me as a lover?")

macrobotic: [MacIntosh + robotic portmanteau ≈ macrobiotic] having to do with robots made by Apple

madrigal: [Fren.] poem with 2-or-3 tercets, of 7-or-11 syllables rhyming (abc)dd or ababcbcc

madvertising: [mad advertising] advertising that takes advantage of public innumeracy by making price appear less high, product quality or popular higher

Magari: describes words which change to another word when a double vowel with an m between is reduced to the vowel: amass (ass), emend (end), homo (ho), limit (lit), stymy (sty), thymy (thy), timing (ting), see Af Jinni

mahakathana: [Sanskrit] ten-to-the-hundred-thirty-third, 10^{133}, long googol

mag-got: [maggot hyphenym] any of the many, pesty inserts that infest the pages of a magazine

magniphobia: [magnification -phobia portmanteau] abnormal fear that the object in the side mirror is much, much closer than it appears

maie: [maize back-formation] corn kernel

major: [maj- mondegreen] describes word beginning with maj- generating a fictitious name, Maj. Esty, Maj. Estik, Maj. Orette, Maj. Goritti, Maj. Uscule

malapropism: [Sheridan's *The Rivals*' Mrs. Malaprop] desirable, desirous;fortunate, fortuitous; humiliation, humility; inflammable, inflammatory; incredible, incredulous; predicate, predict; pretend, portend see bonaprop

maleesh: [paleologism] ignore, forget
Malek's Law: The simpler the idea the greater the complexity with which it will be communicated.
mallmanac: [mall + almanac portmanteau] graphical labyrinth aka Directory
mallum: [paleologism] common sense, understand(ing)
mammothicle: [mammoth + icicle portmanteau] frozen mammoth, used as evidence for catastrophism
man: [Japanese and Sino-Korean] myriad or ten-to-the-fourth, fourplex,10^4
manat: [manatee back-formation] what manater does to a manatee
mandogger: [dog in manger wordle] someone denying to someone else what they cannot use themself
manifold: [daffynition] crease by hand
manufracture: [manufacture + fracture portmanteau] break by hand as with unsliced bread
manunkind: [mankind + unkind mondegreen] more beastly segment of humanity
manurever: [maneuver mondegreen] spread fertilizer
Manx: [Manx cat] curtailed, with last letter or digit deleted
Marchteenth: [March + -teenth compound] octave in mid-March between 13th and 19th
marsoupial: [marsupial + soupy portmanteau] word hidden within a larger one, not discontinuous like a joey or between two like a hiddenym: labo<u>rato</u>ry
masonic: [Perry Mason back-formation] able to manipulate others into spontaneous confessions
mast-headed: [masthead hyphenym] describing a word beginning with mast- but not referring to mast: mastectomy, master, masterpiece, mastic, mastiff, mastodon, masturbation,
mast-ectomy: [mastectomy hyphenym] removing the mast of a ship, radio antenna or forest nuts for swine
mast-turbation: [mast + perturbation portmanteau] shaking of a ship's mast
matchbook: [mondegreen] collection of matchmaker's testimonials
mathemagical: [mathematical + magical portmanteau] math that seems like magic to the uninitiated
mathematician: [Brahmagupta] someone who can solve $x^2 - 92y^2 = 1$ with 1151 and 120
mathsemantics: [Edward MacNeal] semantics of mathematics
matriside: [matricide mondegreen] side of a double bed that the mother sleeps on
maxi-mum: [maximum mondegreen] working, single mother who can do it all, wonder woman
maximin: maximum of minimums
May's Law: Quality of correlation varies inversely to density of control (the fewer the facts, the smoother the curves)
maya: [Sanskrit] mistaken belief that any symbol, any word, any conceptualization, all creation itself is more than a mere representation of Truth
Mayteenth: [May + -teenth compound] octave in mid-May between 13th and 19th
McGee's First Law: [Fibber McGee] It's amazing how long it takes to complete something you're not working on.
McGoon's Law: The likelihood of winning varies inversely to the amount wagered.
meander: chain of words with ending matching beginning: (1) California, Alaska, Arctic, Chicago, Ohio, ...; (2) soon, once, cede, dear, area, each, chat
meanderthal: [meander + Neanderthal portmanteau] wilderness explorer or spelunker
meaning: taking the sum of a number of values and dividing by the number of values
meantime: [mondegreen] early morning, before coffee addicts drink their first cup

meat-headed: meathead hyphenym] describing a word beginning with meat- but not referring to meat: meatus

medling: [meddling mondegreen] young, interfering doctor or intern

mega: [Hugo Steinhaus] two-hexated-to-the-second-power or two-to-the-sixty-five-thousand-five-hundred-thirty-sixth, little sixty-five-thousand-five-hundred-thirty-sixplex, $g(5, 2, 2) = 2^{65,536} > 10^{19,665}$

megalosesquipedalian: describing a large word with 24 letters but less than than ultramegalosesquipedalian (29 letters)

megaloziticorumbatous: [megalosesquipedalian + zitcorumbatous portmanteau] describes 28-letter nonce word

megiston: [Hugo Steinhaus] ten-hexated-to-the-second-power, $g(5, 2, 10)$

mehstcotgotl: [Julia Ward Howe acronym] "Mine eyes have seen the coming of the glory of the Lord."

melon collie: [melancholy mondegreen] sheep dog retrained to guard gourds

memnonyms: [Agamemnonym frag + -nym] n-letter word containing two palindromic trigrams or corresponding (n - 2)-letter word without them

Mencken's Law: Those who can, do; those who can't, teach; (Martin's Extention) those who can't teach, administrate.

Mencken's Metalaw: For every human problem, there is a neat, simple solution which is always wrong.

meng: [Tom Graves from *I Ching*] youthful folly, childish ways, innumeracy

mense: [paleologism] propriety

mental block: [monegreen] from what virtual castles-in-the-air are built

mental telepathy: communication between minds as opposed to abdominal (gut feeling) or cardiac (heart-felt) or optical (eye-to-eye communication) telepathy

meritricious: [meritorious + delicious portmanteau] good for you and good-tasting too

merology: [Lee Sallows, numerology mondegreen] variant of numerology in which the merological value of a number name equals the number

meronym: between two extremes: black < grey < white, convex < flat < concave

Mersenne: power of two's predecessor, $M_n = 2^n -1$

metafiction: self-referencing and so aesthetically distancing fiction

metalalge: [metallage metallage] metallage with sixth and seventh letters exchanged

metallaeg: [metallage metallage] metallage with eighth and nineth letters exchanged

metaphor: "apple of His eye", "flowing with milk and honey", "Fortress","Rock", "Sheild", "thorn in side"**metathesis**: transposition of letters or phonemes: "modren" for "modern"

metaphysical conceit: describing the indescribable by substituting afar-fetched experience

Metcalfe's Law: [Robert Metcalf] "The value of a system grows as approximately the square of the number of users of the system."

metlalage: [metallage metallage] metallage with fourth and fifth letters exchanged

metallgae: [metallage metallage] metallage with seventh and eighth letters exchanged

meteorwright: [meteorite + -wright portmanteau] artist who crafts meteoric material into jewelry

metrognome: [metropolitan gnome portmanteau, metronome mondegreen] small, bearded city dweller

Meyer's Law: "The best thing to do is the most difficult."

microkan: [milli- : micro- :: millikan : ?] probability = 0.0001%

mid-riff: [midriff hyphenym] in the middle of a passage of music

mid-word: [inner/outerword extrapolation] pure word with letters from the middle third of the alphabet (counting from blank as zero), i-to-q:

midderword: [mid-word extrapolation] pure word with letters from the more inner middle of the alphabet, f-to-l: fig, gig, hi, high

middererword: [midderword extrapolation] pure word with letters from the more outer middle of the alphabet, n-to-t: no, not, pot, ton, tot, toot

middestword: [midderword extrapolation] pure word with the letter from the middle of the alphabet (counting from blank as zero), m: mmmm

middleweight: with weight per length between 3 and 6

midword: word formed from the middle of a bookend word: bat (debater), game (ligament), one (money), side (resident), tray (betrayer)

Miksch's Law: "If a string has one end it has two."

Miller's Law: "You can't tell how deep a puddle is until you step into it."

milkdudes: [milkdud + dude portmanteau] two or more milkduds fused together

millillion: [centi- : milli- :: centillion : ?] $10^{3,003}$

millneckstone: [millstone around neck wordle] execution

mincing: softening of too strong oath, blimey (May God blind me), bloody (By our lady), gad (God), gadzooks (By God's hooks, nails), jeez (Jesus), odsbodkins (By God's little Body, the Host), zounds (By Christ's wounds)

ming: [paleologism] stink

mini-mum: [minimum mondegreen] very small mother

minimax: minimum of maximums

miraculous: see Littlewood's Law

mis: [paleologism] disoriented, lost, bewildered

miss-fortune: [≈ misfortune] uncertain outcome of an unmarried woman's search for a husband or of a man's search for an unmarried woman

MIST Law: [man-in-street] The probability of being observed is directly proportional to the stupidity of your action.

mita: [paleologism] with a grain of salt

mitni: [paleologism] policeman

mitocewtpol: [Greville acronym] "Man is the only creature endowed with the power of laughter."

Mnax: [Manx aangram] without tail and with first and second line exchanged

mnemonic: aid to memorizing: "three, two, six times ten-to-six" (megaparsec = 3.26 x 10^6 ly); FACTS (fever, aches, chills, tiredness, sudden onset -symptoms of flu), "When juries lack honor, justice gets forgotten, making criminals miss correcting wrongs.", "When juries lack honor, justice gets forgotten, making criminals." (U. S. bills: Washington ($1), Jefferson ($2), Lincoln ($5), Hamilton ($10), Jackson ($20), Grant ($50), Franklin ($100), McKinley ($500), Cleveland ($1000)), HOMES (Great Lakes: Huron, Ontario, Michigan, Erie, Superior), "My very educated mother just served us noodles." (planets: Mercury, Venus, Earth, Mars, Jupiter, Saturn, Uranus, Neptune.), "Kids prefer cheese over fried green spinach." (toxonomy: kingdom, phylum, class, order, family, genus, species), "Cows Often Sit Down Carefully. Perhaps Their Joints Creak? Persistent Early Oiling Might Prevent Painful Rheumatism. " (geological periods: Cambrian, Ordovician, Silurian, Devonian, Carboniferous, Permian, Triassic, Jurassic, Cretaceous, Paleocene, Eocene, Oligocene, Miocene, Pliocene, Pleistocene, Recent)

mninge: [paleologism] great number

mo: [H. G. Wells] great gross, $12^3 = 1,728$
Mo: [Manx Moo] quintuply curtailed
modownuth: [down in mouth wordle] not well
modulation: operation of evaluating n as if only a remainder when n is divided by n', symbolized with a percent sign between them, n%n'
mofootuth: [foot in mouth wordle] unretractable *faux pa*
mok: [from Arthur C. Clark's M0K] mystery of the zeroth kind, no mystery at all
mokita: [New Guinean Kiriwina] truth everybody knows but which is left unexpressed to the point of eventually becoming unthinkable
molecule: [David Morice] analysis of letters' connections in non-eodermdromes, symbolized by kissing circles becoming concentric with each letter use
Mondale's Law: [Walter Mondale] "If you think you understand, you are actually hopelessly confused."
mondegreen: ["laid him on the green" = Lady Mondegreen] misheard and reinterpreted word or phrase
mongie: [paleologism] dull, stupid; dirty, nasty
monoalphabetical: words whose letters are in alphabetical order:addest, Achior acknow, acorsy, Adelops, adempt, adipsy, aegilops, agnosy, almost, beefily, befist, begirt, begorry, beknow, bijoux, billowy, biopsy, cestuy, chintz, deflux, dehors, dehort, Deimos, deinos, diluvy, dimpsy, egilops, ghostly
monochromatic: [resistor code] repdigit-like
monoconsonantal: describes word with just one consonant: alleluia, asses, baobob
monogram: work using just one letter: poems collected in *Alphabetical Anthology* ed. by Joyce Holland
monorhymed: poem rhyming a...a: "Mary had a little lamb, who was as happy as a clam and through ev'ry door that Mary'd slam Mary's lamb would surely scram."
monosyllabic: word with just one syllable: screeched, strengths
monovoweled: describes word with just one (repeated) vowel: banana, defenselessness, primitivistic, polo, untrustful, syzygy
monstroziticorumbatous: [monstrous + zitcorumbatous portmanteau] describes 22-letter nonce word
Moo: [Moorean Moorean] quadruply curtailed
Moor: [Manx Moore] triply curtailed
Moorean: [Moore + -an] Manx Manx, like Moore's limericks, doubly line-curtailed
moralistic fallacy: confusing what ought to be for what is
Moravec's paradox: Logical thought is hard for humans and easy for computers, but picking a screw from a box of screws is an unsolved problem.
moregami: [more + origami portmanteau] folding of facial tissues that allows them to methodically emerge from the box just one more at a time
morsynonyms: [Morse + synonym] words that translate into the same Morse code dot-dash sequence, dash-dot-dot-dash-dash-dash = do = neo = team
Mosher's Law: Retiring too soon is better than retiring too late.
mort: [paleologism] honest, old-fashioned person
motte-and-bailey fallacy: bait and switch definism
mrevest: [Magna res est vocis est silentii temperamentum. acronym] The great thing is to know when to speak and when to keep quiet.

mu: [Japanese] answer to question both unanswerable and, if questioner had more understanding, unaskable

Muir's Law: [aka Commoner's 1st] Everything is connected to everything else.

multi-ply: [multiply hyphenym] premium quality toilet paper

mumble-jumble: [mumbo-jumbo mondegreen] something heard with difficulty and understood with greater difficulty

mumbleteen: indeterminate number between thirteen and nineteen, $13 \leq n \approx 16 \leq 19$

mumblety: indeterminate multiple of ten, between twenty and ninety, $20 \leq n \approx 55 \leq 90$

mumbleplex: indeterminate power of ten, 10^n

Munnecke's Law: If you don't say it, they can't repeat it.

munum: [mynonym + -num(ber)] palindromic number

munoonum: palinddromic, double-yolked palindromic number

Muphry's Law: If you write anything criticizing, editing or proofreading, there will be a fault of some kind in what you have written.

Murphy's Law: [Edward A. Murphy, Jr.] "If anything can go wrong, it will.", aka 4th Law of Thermodynamics: "If the probability of success is not almost one, then it is almost zero."

muryou: [Jap.] ten-to-the-sixty-eighth, sixty-eightplex, 10^{68}

muryougasha: [kou : kougasha :: muryou : ?] ten-to-the-eighty-eighth, eighty-eightplex, 10^{88}

mush room: [mushroom charade] large storage place for baby food

musical: describes words with the sol-fa syllables (do, re, mi, fa, so, la, ti): ado, ala, are, blah, do, doe, dog, dot, ere, fab, fad, fan, far, fat, fax, ire, ...

mustgo: [musty, must go] malodorous refrigerated food

myanalysis: [urinalysis mondegreen antonym] correct conclusion as apposed to others'

myeambil: [Mt 11:30 acronym] "My yoke's easy and my burden is light."

mypaq: [acronym] "Mind your P's and Q's."

mynynym: [myny- + -nym] palindromic portmanteau made by combining a prefix or suffix and its ananym

myriad: [Greek] ten thousand, 10^4

mythistory: [myth + history portmanteau $\approx$ mystery] myth that's something like myth or v. v.

N - 1 Law: "The last of a set is the most difficult to find."

N - 7 method: [reverse of Jean Lescure's N + 7 method] reconstructing a text before revision by N + 7 method, substituting noun seven ahead in dictionary, "To be or not to be that is the qualm.", see W ± n

n-invariant: describes words which have an n only in the 14th place: autosuggestion, beautification, businessperson, bipolarization, bowdlerization, capitalization

naagram: [anagram metallage] anagram with first and second letters exchanged

naav: ["Natura abhorret a vacuo." acronym] Nature abhors a vacuum.

nade: one of the words making up an alternade, binade, trinade, quaternade, quinade: "shoe" or "cold" in "schooled", see frag

nadi: [Balinese] temporarily living in an altered state of consciousness as do the gifted, inspired

nagabala: [Sanskrit] ten-to-the-twenty-fifth, twenty-fiveplex, 10^{25}

Nagari: describes words which change to another word when a double vowel with an n between is reduced to the vowel: anarch (arch), dining (ding), mini (mi), pining (ping), sunup (sup), un-unique (unique), wining (wing), see Af Jinni

nagivate: [nag + navigate] criticize driver rather than helping with navigation

nagram: [beheaded anagram] transdeletion with a letter deleted and rest transposed, see andagram

nahuta: [Sanskrit] ten-to-the-twenty-eighth, twenty-eightplex, 10^{28}

namesake: [mondegreen] reason that fathers prefer sons who could pass on the surname

name-thing problem: [Jean Piaget] difficulty in distinguishing name of thing from thing

namedropping: [name + birddropping portmanteau] riddle that asks a pseudo-question incorporating a proper name: Was Robert Frost bitten? How much did Hemming weigh?

namenesia: [name anmesia portmanteau] forgetting a person's name, see Chatsby

nan: ["nunt aut numquam" acronym] now or never

nany: [beheaded and curtailed ananym] describing transdeletion in which word is terminally deleted and reversed: rebirth = tribe

nanum: [beheaded ananum] number reversed and beheaded, R(n/10)

nanym: beheaded ananym: stinky = knits

napjerk: sudden convulsion of the body just as one is about to doze off

napsack: [beheaded knapsack] pillowcased pillow

napture: [nap + rapture portmanteau] fantastically refreshing short sleep break

narrow: describes letters with both ascenderless and descenderless (a, c, e, m, n, o, r, s, u, v, w, x, z): ace, more-so, overnumerousnesses

nasal: m, n, ng

naughtiness: percentage of zeroes (naughts) in a number's digits

nayuta: [Jap. and Sin-Korean] ten-to-the-sixtieth, sixtyplex, 10^{60}

nayutagasha: [kou : kougasha :: nayuta : ?] ten-to-the-eighteenth, eightplex, 10^{80}
-the-eighteenth, 10^{80}

nearfetched: [farfetched back-formation] incredibly credible

néblo: [D'ni] twenty-five-to-the-fifteenth, not-so-little thirtyplex, 25^{15} = 931,322,574,615,478,515,625

necomancy: [neco + necromancy portmanteau] trying to determine the future with thin candy wafers

nedid: ["Noli equi dentes inspicere donati." acronym] Don't look a gift horse in the mouth.

neep-neep: computer addict

Nef's Law: [Evvie Nef] "There is a solution to every problem; the only difficulty is finding it."

nefriended: [friend in need wordle] helpmate

negli-gent: [negligent hyphenym, negligee gentleman portmanteau] man who "accidentally" wears lingerie

neid: ["Nullus est instar domus." acronym] There's no place like home

neighbor: letter or number one higher or lower high in alphabet or sequence, f(n ± 1)

nélen: [D'ni] twenty-five-to-the-thirteenth, not-so-little twenty-sixplex, 25^{13} = 1,490,116,119,384,765,625

neltmunapp: ["Nullus est liber tam malus ut non aliqua parte prosit." acronym] No book's so bad that it's not profitable on some part.

némel: [D'ni] twenty-five-to-the-fourteenth, not-so-little twenty-eightplex, 25^{14} = 37,252,902,984,619,140,625

neonphancy: [neon + infancy portmanteau] struggling of a fluorescent light bulb to come to life

neontology: [paleontology back-formation] study of newly found "extinct" creatures

nepainck: [pain in neck wordle] nuisance

Nepalese: aka panlipogrammatic, describing poem variation with first and/or last 5 lines missing as described by: "There once was a man from Nepal Whose limericks had no lines at all. Since no space they took, He published a book With an infinite number in all."

néra: [D'ni] twenty-five-to-the-eleventh, not-so-little twenty-twoplex, 25^{11} = 2,384,185,791,015,625

nés: [D'ni] twenty-five-to-the-twelfth, not-so-little twenty-fourplex, 25^{12} = 59,604,644,775,390,625

nesh: [paleologism] spring grass; delicate, gentle, kindly, fastidious, dainty, timid

nesting: repeated substitution of an operation as in the third-order nesting to the sixty-fourth in Graham's number; quotations within quotations ("Once upon a time a story began 'Once upon a time ...'.")

new-fangled: [newfangled back-formation] with never-used fangles

newtrition: [new + nutrition portmanteau] ever-changing determination of what food is good for you

niarogaarom: [Longfellow acronym] "Nature is a revelation of God; art a revelation of man."

nibfepov: [Horace acronym] "Nothing is beautiful from every point of view."

nikhedonia: [paleologism] thrill of anticipated victory or success

nimbecile: [nimble + imbecile portmanteau] physically quick though mentally slow person like Jack who needs to be told not to jump into the fire

nimber: [Nim number portmanteau] alternate subgroup of games to numbers that add as in Nim, in base two without carrying

nimble: [homonym and/or synonym chain using law of undistributed middle] beehive = bee-holder (beholder) = spectator (specked tater) = rotten potato, bribe = consent rate (concentrate) = think = reckon = figure =shape = fashion = style (stile) = gate (gait) = pace = walk, pretty girl = belle (bell) = ringer = dinner = meal = flour (flower), ruled sheet = ink-lined plane (inclined plane) = slope up (slow pup) = lazy dog, sore = saw in halves = whole (hole), an ice box = a nice box = a box of candy = sweetmeat (sweet meet) = pretty girls = belles (bells) = diving = sport = gay blade = grass = hay (hey) = exclamation = surprise = catch unaware = underwear; see chain conundrum

nineight: [eight + nine portmanteau] eight/nine

nineighteen: eighteen + nineteen portmanteau] eighteen/nineteen

ninety-nines: $10^{91} - 1 = 9[10^{90}/9]$

ninnahuta: [Sanskrit] ten-to-the-thirty-fifth, thirty-fiveplex, 10^{35}

nir: ["Nihil ad res." acronym] Nothing to do with the point

nirabbuda: [Sanskrit] ten-to-the-sixty-third, sixty-threeplex, 10^{63}

niravadya: [Sanskrit] ten-to-the-forty-fifth, forty-fiveplex, 10^{45}

nitat: [2 Cor 6:2 acronym] "Now is the appointed time."

nitmoi: [Aesop acronym] "Necessity is the mother bof invention."

nixonym: [Nixon + -nym] word, like NIXON, with only upside-down letters, i. e., H, I, N, O, S, X or Z: hi, his, hiss, I, in, inn, is, no, on, Oz, shin, sis, six, son, zoo

no-how: [know-how mondegreen] combination of inexperience and lack of education

no-pun: [from "no pun intended"] unintentional pun

no-showoff: chronically late person of overachiever, usually overachiever parent

noh: [nose back-formation] small nostril-like hole

non-vicinal: word with not all letters alphabetical neighbors: vicinal

nonce: word coined for a particular occasion

noncrashing: [David Silverman] words with no letter in the same position: bra, car, dew, ebb, fly, gnu, ...; ammo, czar, etch, fizz, husk, ikon, knew, ...; angst, bluff, drink, ethyl, fjord, gizmo, lynch,...; asthma, cystic, embryo, freeze, guffaw, hiccup, ...

nonet: poem with $9 + 8 + 7 + 6 + 5 + 4 + 3 + 2 + 1 = 45$ syllables rhyming $a^2b^2c^2d^3$

nonina: 81-verse quenina with spirally permutated verse pattern: 123456789, 918273645, 594168327, 752934816, 671582493, 369741258, 835629174, 487315962, 246897531 [*Etoffe* by Jacques Rouband, 1974]

nonosecond: [no-no + nanosecond portmanteau] instant between making a big mistake and being able to do anything about it

nonyms: [Agamemnonnym frag] n-letter word containing one palindromic trigram or corresponding (n - 1)-letter word without it: fife, fie

nopo: ["Non omnia possumus omnes." acronym] Not all of us're able to do everything.

noqnae: ["Non omne quod nitet aurum est." acronym] Not all that glitters is gold

nosetalgia: [nose + nostalgia portmanteau] describing fond remini-scent-triggered memories

not-so-little: [little back-formation] reduced by dividing by power-of-two factors

nozzea: [nausea + nozzle portmateau] upset at prospect of drinking water from a garden hose

nrisgwanse: [acronym] "No rule is so general which admits not some exception."

nuckle: [beheaded knuckle] scraped knuckle

nuddle: [paleologism] walk quickly with head bent down

nugon: [nu + -gon] polygon formed from N-like triple line segments

num: [A. K. Dewdney] number with too few significant digits to be useful, see pure math

number: mathematical expression that numbs the minds of the mathematically challenged, see killion

number abuse: use of math to confuse, mislead or terrorize

number filtering: [John Allen Paulos] removing vital number from calculation

number inflation: [A. K. Dewdney] unbelievably large number, usually by adding together overlapping categories

number numbness: [Douglas Hofstadter] inability to appreciate very large or very small numbers, as in thinking the difference between a million and a billion is just one letter out of seven rather than one out of a thousand

number sense: [Lynn Arthur Steen] ability to think both abstractly and practically, see approximating, guesstimating

number terrorism: number abuse used to terrorize

number tree: family-tree-like connections between numbers related by transaddition or transdeletion

numberddrome: [words : palinddrome :: numbers : ?] aka rebmun number, "double-yolked" numberdrome with repeated central digit

numberdrome: [number palindrome portmanteau] aka rebmu number, number reading the same forward and backward

numeral: symbolic representation of a number

numerate: [John Allen Paulos] able to understand basic math both abstractly and practically

numerical unit: word used in number names, like one and hundred in one hundred

numerogenealogy: [numerology genealogy portmanteau] study of number trees

numerologology: wordplay with number names (arithmonyms)

numerosity: [Brian Butterworth] number as collection rather than abstraction

nurae: ["Non uno die Roma aedificata est." acronym] things take time

nurt: [paleologism] current, trend, course
nushellt: [in nut shell wordle] summarized
nutjob: squirrel's occupation
nymber: [nym- + number] arithmonym which can be ambiguously read as another number as a wordnum or alphadecimal
nymeral: Roman numeral which can be read ambiguously as æquicalculation or wordnum or alphadecimal
o-a-sis: [oasis mondegreen] expression used when learning one's newborn sibling is a girl
o-invariant: describes words with o only in the 15th place: alphabetization, acclimatization, characterization, crystallization, declassification, demagnetization, depressurization
O-keili: describes words with only o as vowel: bloodshot, blossom, colon, comfort, cocoon, doctor, Mormon, polo, pooh, popcorn, school, tomorrow, too, toot, voodoo
oafficial: [oaf +official portmanteau] public official who acts like an oaf
oagaag: [Dickens acronym] "Once a gentleman, always a gentleman."
oblitherate: [obliterate + blither portmanteau] defeat one's opponent by exposing his/her idiocy
Obvious Law: It only seems as though you mustn't be deceived by appearances.
obviously: taught in a previous, and not to be repeated, lesson
ocke: [acronym] "one cannot know everything."
Octember: [October + November portmanteau] 61 days between September and December
octisograms: eight words with no letters in common: adz, cwm, fob, jug, nth, rip, sky, vex
octuplet: [septuplet extrapolation] changing one word into another seven letters at a time
ocurrencia: [Spanish] sudden, unobvious, bright idea or witty remark
odd: one in modulo two, $2n + 1 = 1(\bmod 2) = 1\%2$; describing word with odd wordnum product, i. e., containing only the odd letters: a, c, e, g, i, k, m, o, q, s, u, w, or y; ace = 15
odder: with odd number of prime factors, like $3(5)7 = 105$
oddernate: [odd + alternate portmanteau] with digits alternating odd and even
oddition: [odd + addition portmanteau] addition of odd numbers
odormatopeia: coining a word from the smell associated with it: stinkbug
Odo's numbers: [Odo of Châteauroux, 1372] number of fallen angels, $2^2 3^3 11^2 101^2 = 133{,}306{,}668$; unfallen, $2^3 3^3 11^2 101^2 = 266{,}613{,}336$; total, $2^2 3^4 11^2 101^2 = 399{,}920{,}004$
odormotopeia: [odor + onomatopeia portmanteau] naming of something from its smell, like skink bug
odwys: [acronym] "O death where's your sting."
oel: ["ora et labora" acronym] work and pray
off-beat: [offbeat hyphenym] unorthodox policing to throw the criminals off
oggin: [noggin elesion] small melon
ogha: [Sanskrit] ten-to-the-fiftieth, fiftyplex, 10^{50}
ogring: [ogle + ogre portmanteau] looking too long at ugliness
ogtutlfhig: [Ps 107:1] "O give thanks to the Lord, for He is good."
oh-oh: [double oh] informal name for double zero (00), lazy eight (∞), symbols for infinity
oholene: [hole in one wordle] rare accomplishment
oinbji: [Voltaire acronym] "Originality is nothing but judicious imitation."
oinkment: [oink + government portmanteau] rule by male chauvinists
ointflyment: [fly in ointment wordle] one flaw that spoils whole
oku: [Jap.] myllion, ten-to-the-eighth, eightplex, 10^8
olc: [0LC grammanym] zero-level consciousness, unconsciousness

olympi-ad: [olympiad mondegreen, olympics advertisement portmanteau] commercial shown during Summer or Winter Games

omega: Ω, ultimate infinity

Omish: [Percy Mo + -ish] quintuply curtailed and reversed

ommap: [Aesop acronym] "One man's meat's another's poison."

ommp: [Omnia mea mecum porto. acronym] All that's mine I carry.

omnivia: [3 : all :: trivia : ?] connection between everything

omonym: [beheaded homonym] word that becomes its own homonym when an initial letter is added: cent, hole, isle, lama, nap, nave, need, new, nickers, night, nit, Nome, not, our, salter, rap, rest, retch, right, rite, rote, see shomonym

onalosi: [isolano anaym] aka friendly word

oneare: [in one ear wordle] unlisteningly

onetic: [phonetically beheaded phonetic] word with its initial phoneme removed: basalt (assualt)

onna: [acronym] oh no! not again!

onomastics: wordplay with names

onomatopeia: basing word upon sound: meong (Indonesian), meov (Serbian), meow (English), miagolio (Italian), miaou (French), miau (Finnish, German, Hungarian, Lithuanian, Polish, Portuguese, Romanian, Spanish), miauw (Afrikaans), miauwen (Dutch), miyav (Turkish), mjaullin (Albanian)

onymous: unonymous antonym] with not all secret ballots in agreement

onumastics: [onomastics + number portmanteau] wordplay with number names

ooglified: describes a word whose vowel sound is changed to oo: about (aboot), cigarette (cigaroot), shit (shoot), Skandinavian (Skandinoovian), snout (snoot), ugly (oogly)

oogol: [10^{100} : googol :: 10^{∞} : ?, beheaded googol] name for the angelic number, one followed by an infinite number of zeroes

ooiapohv: [Alcott paraphrase acronym] "One's outlook is a part of his/her virtue."

Oomish: [Percy Moo + -ish] quadruply curtailed then reversed

oop: [beheaded loop, Alley Oop] loop and then behead

OOPO: [out-of-place object] something not where it's expected to be

oopunling: [enloopuing : loopuning :: loopuning : ?] forming (51234, 561234, 5671234, . ..) anagrams by moving 4 times the initial letters to tail

oopling: [ploo : oplo :: oplo : ?] forming (23451, 345612, 4567123, etc.) anagrams by moving the final letter to the initial position 4 times

Oor: [Percy Roo] triply curtailed, reversed, curtailed again, then reversed again

oosoom: [Barnabe Googe acronym] "Out of sight, out of mind."

operadical: [operatic + radical portmanteau] unconventional opera singer, not necessarily a prima donna

oploing: [loop : ploo :: ploo : ?] forming (2341, 34512, 456123, .. .) anagrams by 3 times moving the final letter to the initial position

opunlo: [loopun : oopunl :: oopunl : ?] form (612345, 6712345, 67812345, etc.) anagrams by moving initial letters 5 times to tail

oproqoropro: [ABCD : OPQR :: abracadabra : ?] nonsense word like abracadabra

oqeiri: [O quantum est in rebus inane! acronym] O, how much futility in the world!

oquilt: [ocult + quilt portmanteau] patchwork flying carpet

Or: [Percy Ro] triply curtailed, reversed, doubly curtailed and then reversed again

ord: beheaded word

Ore: [Percy Ero] doubly curtailed and reversed, then double curtailed and reversed again
Orion's Law: Everything breaks down.
orthinology: [ornithology Spoonerism] substitution of one heteronym for another
OS-graphable: [octogon-square, Leonard Gordon] word graphable as if on octogon-square tiling: horseshoers
Osborn's Law: Variables won't; constants aren't.
ose: [morose mondegreen] long, morbid, miserable ballad
oss: [O sancta simplicitas! acronym] Oh, holy simplicity!
osteopornosis: [osteoporosis + porn portmanteau] hardening of pornographic addiction
othwaskpe: [Goethe acronym] "Only the heart without a stain knows perfect ease."
oticwiir: [Pope acronym] "One thing is clear; whatever is is right."
otnim: [H. G. Wells acronym] "Our true nationality is mankind."
otom: ["O tempera, o mores!" acronym] grief over declining morals
otoh: [acronym] on the other hand
ottava rima: 8 verses in iambic pentameter rhyming ababcc
ouijanym: [ouija word] word like ouija divisible into bilingual homonyms: Andy, demisemi, fisnoga, heel, lathe, mime, oro, pillicock, reindeer, toad, yet
our-bitrate: [arbitrate mondegreen] bit coin exchange compared to competitor's
ourhour: couple's private time alone together
ouroboronym: [ouroboros + -nym] word with identical ends: Church, claustrophobic, deride, edified, edited, educated, enliven, entertainment, enticement, entrancement, escapes, esquires, estates, fireproof, gerrymandering, growing, halleluiah, headache, illuminati, ingesting, ingrowing, insulin, knapsack, logical, memorandum, orator, photograph, restores, sense, shellfish, teammate, temperate, terminate, that, verve, yesterday
ouroboros: word worm that turns back on itself at ends: 1 (30) 2 (60) 3 = any, cup, paw, toe, ...; 2 (60) 2 (60) 2 = bow; 1 (60) 3 (120) 1 (60) 3 (120) = coot; 3 (60) 3 (60) 3 (60) 3 = taxi
ourus: [backformed from missouri, pl. ouri] describes word beginning with mis- pronounced ms- [miz-], see issippus
out-going: [mondegreen] exiting, leaving
out-rank: [out-rank mondegreen] smell worse than
out-trigger: [outrigger mondegreen] something that prompts out-goingness
outercom: [intercom antonym] megaphone, bullhorn
outerword: [outword extrapolation] pure word from the outer third of the alphabet (counting from blank as zero), r-to-z: rust, rut, strut, tut-tut
outestword: [outerword extrapolation]: pure word from the letters more outer than outerwords, u-to-z: tut-tut
outword: [outward mondegreen] pure word with letters from the outer alphabet, n-to-z: nonsupports, ports, supports
ova(enca): ["omnia vincit amor (et nos cedamus amori)" acronym] love conquers all, let us yield to Love
ovalation: [oval + ovation portmanteau] good news from the president's oval office
ovaluable: [oval + valuable portmanteau] quite worth having like a golden egg and even more so the goose that lays them
over-charge: [overcharge hyphenym] botch a cavalry maneuver like in Crimea
over-headed: [overhead hyphenym] describes a word beginning with over- not referring to over: overt, overture
overbyte: [over- + byte ≈ overbite] too much information

overgeneralization: fallacy of basing conclusion on little evidence
overlobe: [overload + earlobe mondegreen] add too much ear-piercing, earring erring
overrounding: rounding and then re-rounding or rounding more than to significant digit
ownstewjuice: [stew in own juice wordle] reap the rotten fruits of one's deeds
oxymoron: juxtaposition of seemingly contradictory words: educational television, faint praise, hateful good, jumbo shrimp, military intelligence, moral majority, old news, pretty ugly, random order, student teacher, sweet sorrow
p-devoiced: describes a word whose p changed to a b: pack (back), pad (bad), pan (ban), par (bar), pass (bass), pat (bat), pay (bay), pee (bee)
padlock: word formed from beginning of one word and ending of another, not a portmanteau, with or without chain: nor<u>ther</u> + <u>ther</u>mal = normal, pad<u>re</u> + <u>retrench</u> + <u>trenchant</u> + <u>anthem</u> + <u>hemlock</u> = padlock, see combination
padma: [Sanskrit] ten-to-the-thirty-second, thirty-twoplex, 10^{32}
paduma: [Sanskrit] ten-to-the-hundred-nineteenth, hundred-nineteenplex, 10^{119}
Pagari: describes words which change to another word when a double vowel with a p between is reduced to the vowel: apart (art), lipid (lid), piping (ping), propose (prose), riping (ring), wiping (wing), see Af Jinni
paiedog: [Francis J. Spellman] "Pray as if everything depends on God."
pair-o'-dime shift: [paradigm shift mondegreen] what happens when twenty cents changes hands
pair-'o-docs: [paradox mondegreen] two doctors in consultation on one patient
pair-ring: [pairing mondegreen] one of a set of two rings, for example, engagement and wedding rings
pairogram: two-anagram phrase: actor's co-star, American cinerama, Elvis lives, married admirer
paisle: [paisley back-formation] teardrop-shaped microörganism that inspired
pakoti: [Sanskrit] ten-to-the-fourteenth, fourteenplex, 10^{14}
pale-eontology: [paleontology hyphenym] study of fossils recognizing how woefully meager they are and how many OOPOs (out-of-place objects) are among what is left
paleologism: [neologism antonym] once new, but then neglected, word
palinddrome: aka double-yolked palindrome, palindrome with double central letter
palindrome: [Abbess Ebba] word that reads the same backward: boob, civic, dad, deified, dewed, eke, gag, kayak, Mayalayam, minim, mum, noon, peep, racecar, redder, re-divider, refer, re-paper, reviver, semi-times, sexes
palindromic phrase: phrase whose string reads the same backward: "ablata at alba"(Lat. "banished but blameless"), "liad ded dail" (Welsh "holy blind father"); "A man, a plan, Panama!" (George Washington Goethals), "a mock coma"; "dessert stressed"; "Nell, Edna, Ann, Ahab, Eric, Art, Leon, Mike, Ed, Dee, Kim, Noel, Traci, Reba, Hanna and Ellen."; "never odd or even"; "no lemons, no melon"; "no stetson"; "remarkable Elba Kramer"; "ruffled elf fur"; "too hot to hoot"; "wet stew"
palindromic sentence: sentence whose string reads the same backward: "Si nummi immunis." (Lat. "Pay your fee and you go free."); "Lewd I did live & evil did I dwel." (first in English, John Taylor), "Able was I ere I saw Elba."; "Ana, nab a banana."; "Are we not drawn forward to a new era?"; "Bob's partner entraps Bob."; "Dennis and Edna sinned."; "Don't nod."; "Draw, O coward!"; "Evade Dave." "Even an Eve!"; "I, man, am regal; a German am I."; "Madam, I'm Adam."; "Mix a maxim."; "No, it is open on one position."; "Nurse, I spy gypsies; run!"; "Pull up if I pull up."; "Sit on a potato pan, Otis."; "So many dynamos!"; "Stop spots.";

"Sums are not set as a test on Erasmus."; "Tim, as demanded, named Sam 'it.'"; "Too far, Edna, we wander afoot!", "Was it a rat I saw?"

palindromics: combining forty pairs of ananyms generates ten thousand 8-word palindromic sentences: #1 "Emit bus, drab bats stab bard, sub time." ... #9,999 "Wed rats, ten tips spit net, star dew.",

[0] Emit	[0] bus,	[0] drab	[1] bats	[1] stab	[0] bard,	[0] sub	[0] time.
[1] Edit	[1] deer,	[1] live	[1] buns	[1] snub	[1] evil,	[1] reed	[1] tide.
[2] Doom	[2] loot,	[2] mad	[2] naps	[2] span	[2] dam,	[2] tool	[2] mood.
[3] Flog	[3] gats,	[3] raw	[3] nuts	[3] stun	[3] war,	[3] stag	[3] golf.
[4] Mar	[4] gum,	[4] regal	[4] pals	[4] slap	[4] lager,	[4] gum	[4] ram.
[5] Nab	[5] part,	[5] sleek	[5] pans	[5] snap	[5] keels,	[5] trap	[5] ban.
[6] Pat	[6] pit,	[6] snug	[6] paws	[6] swap	[6] guns,	[6] tip	[6] tap.
[7] Spot	[7] pool,	[7] sore	[7] pins	[7] snip	[7] eros,	[7] loop	[7] gut.
[8] Tug	[8] rail,	[8] straw	[8] pots	[8] stop	[8] warts,	[8] liar	[8] gut.
[9] Wed	[9] rats,	[9] ten	[9] tips	[9] spit	[9] net,	[9] star	[9] dew.

palm reader: [mondegreen] vacationer relaxing with a good book under a palm tree

panamaramic: [Panama panoramic portmanteau] referring to the many variations of Leigh Mercer's Panama palindrome: A lab, a crab, a bar: cabala. A man, a petal, a parade, cedar, a palate: Panama., A man, a post, a fare, salad, a laser, a fatso: Panama.

pandagram: palindromic andagram

pangram: sentence containing whole alphabet: "'Pyrzqxgl, Joe Bkfptll!' said Mxyzptl.", "John P. Brady, give me a black walnut box of quite fairsize." (46), "Pack my box with five dozen liquor jugs." (32), "The quick brown fox jumps over the lazy dog." (35),"Quick wafting zephyrs vex bold Jim." (29), "Waltz, bad nymph, for quick jigs vex." (28, j = i, v = u) Ezra 7:21 (j = i), see isopangram

pangramania: aka Hjelmqvist-Gryb-Zock-Pfund-Wax syndrome ["The Syndrome", named for Prof. Hjelmqvist, speech therapist Alexander Gryb, psycholinguist Friedrich Zock, their assistant Mr. Pfund and Dr. Edward Wax] aka OCPD (obsessive-compulsion pangrammic disorder)

panoramic: number name with one through nine's letters (e, f, g, h, i, n, o, r, s, t, u, v, w, x): twenty-three thousand, five hundred sixty-eight

pantonym: palindromic antonym, like eye

pantitular: [all-title] nothing but the title repeated over and over: Ron Padgett's "Nothing in That Drawer"

pantsants: [ants in pants wordle] fidgety

pantun: [Malayan] poem with four lines rhyming abab

panvocal: word with all 5 (or 6) vowels: abstemious, arsenious, authorize, behaviour, cauliflower, crematorium, efficacious, equation, facetious, frumentarious, graciousness, gregarious, inoculate, lapideous, mendacious, nefarious, ostentatious, precarious, simultaneous, subordinate, tenacious, unsociable, veracious, vexatious, voluntariness;

abstemiously, arseniously, cauliflowery, efficaciously, equationy, facetiously, frumentariously, gregariously, lapideously, mendaciously, nefariously, ostentatiously, precariously, questionably, simultaneously, tenaciously, veraciously, vexatiously

Papagiannis' Law: Absence of evidence's not evidence of absence.

papallege: [pataphysics : patallege :: papaphysics : ?] anagram with four-letter exchange

papaphysics: [metaphysics : pataphysics :: pataphysics : ?] science of the unobservable, unthinkable, unimaginable, beyond physics, metaphysics, or pataphysics, theology: God the Father (Papa)

paperwait: [paperweight mondegreen] time spend in anticipation of delivery of the morning newspaper

paplladseo: [Lawrence Sterne acronym] "Pain and pleasure, like light and darknes, succeed each other."

paradoxical: word made smaller or shorter by adding letters or longer by deleting letters: he, ma, or; ale, all, her, hot, ore, she; male, mall, sale, shot, sore, sort; shore, short; sorter; belonger, longeron, oblonger; prolonger

paradoxy: [paradox + orthodoxy] belief system based upon paradoxes

paragoge: addition of letter or syllable to end of word: "bananana"

paragram: printer's error in a letter

pararhyme: with consonants of syllable but not vowel rhymed

parchtment: [parched + parchment portmanteau] state of being very thirsty

Paris-sight: [parasite mondegreen] anything seen from atop the Eiffel tower pariscope

Parkinson's Laws: [C. Northcote Parkinson] (1) Work expands to fill the time available for its completion; the thing to be done swells in perceived importance and complexity in a direct ratio with the time to be spent in its completion. (2) Expenditures rise to meet income. (3) Expansion means complexity; and complexity decay. (4) The number of people in any working group tends to increase regardless of the amount of work to be done. (5) If there is a way to delay an important decision the good bureaucracy, public or private, will find it. (6) Science's progress's inversely proportional to the number of journals published.

parody: includes both heteroparody and autoparody, used to enlarge dimensions of work(s) with passwords, references, tokens, that are not too obvious: [by Lewis Carroll of "Against Idleness and Mischief" by Dr. Isaac Watts] "How doth the little crocodile (busy bee) Improve his (each) shining tail (hour), And pour the waters of the Nile (gather honey all the day) On every golden scale (From every opening flower).", [by Lewis Carroll of "The Star" by Jane Taylor] "Twinkle, twinkle, little bat! (star) How I wonder what your at! (you are) Up above the would you fly (so high) Like a tea tray (diamond) in the sky."

paronomasia: aka punning, juxtapositioning of ideas for humorous effect: "You can lead a horticulture, but you can't make her think.", "The squaw on the hippopotamus is equal to the sons of the squaws on the other two hides.", "The wise know the whys."

paronomania: [paromonasia + mania portmanteau] abnormal desire to juxtaposition ideas for humorous effect

parthenym: [mis- mondegreen, ≈ parthenon] unmarried woman's beauty or talent contest title, Miss Fit, Miss Hap, Miss Shun, Miss Judge, Miss Match, Miss Shape, Miss Steak, Miss Treat, Miss Tress

Pascal's Law: [Blase Pascal] The intelligent with originality see others'.

past-tense: [past tense hyphenym] now mellowed

past-your-eyes: [pasteurize mondegreen] moving too fast to see, legerdemain

pastorize: [pasteurize mondegreen] put priest into role of pastor of a parish

pataphysics: [physics : metaphysics :: metaphysics : ?] beyond physic or metaphysics
patallege: [metaphysics : pataphysics :: metallege : ?] anagram with three-letter exchange, like eat and ate
path-logical: [path + logical hyphenym ≈ path'logical] always choosing the right way
pathetic fallacy: attributing humanity to inanimate
pathfwig: [1 Th 5:21 acronym] "Prove all things; hold fast what is good."
patl: [Thomas Southberne acronym] "Pity's akin to love."
Patton's Law: A good plan today is better than a perfect one tomorrow.
patriotic: describes number name with USA in it: thousand
patriside: [patricide mondegreen] side of the double bed a father sleeps on
pawast: [James Russell Lowell acronym] "Pride and weakness are Siamese twins."
pawnshop: [mondegreen] seek to buy replacement pawns for one's chess set
Pe: [Moor Percy] reversed and then triply curtailed
peacemeal: [piecemeal mondegreen] peace offering of a meal offered during wartime
pebtib: ["Prejor est bello timor ipse belli." acronym] worse than war is the fear of war
pedlock: [peddle + wedlock portmanteau] condition of a bicycle pedal wedging itself against the kickstand
Peer's Law: The solution to a problem changes the problem, but cannot solve it.
pelf: [paleologism] money, riches
pen name: name printed on a gift pen as advertising for the giver
pentapaul: [Paul Linebarger] poem of just five rhyming words, see haikuization
Per: [Moorean Percy] reversed and then doubly curtailed
Perc: [Manx Percy] reversed and then curtailed
percussive maintenance: [≈ preventive maintenance] "repairing" a machine by giving it a good whack
Percyan: [Percy + -an] line ananym, as in J. A. Lindon's limerick: "That things were not worse was a mercy! You read bottom line first Since he wrote all reversed. He did every job arsy-versy. A very odd poet was Percy!"
perfictionist: [perfectionist + fiction] fiction reader with exacting standards
peripety: action with effect opposite to intention
periphrasis: roundabout manner of saying something
permutational: with verse readable in any order
perrywrinkle: [Perry + wrinkle portmanteau ≈ periwinkle] clue that puts a new twist on a criminal investigation
persistence: count of how many times it takes to reach the one-digit root of a number
persistent: [Robert Ripley] aka cyclical, retaining the same sequence of digits with multiplication
perverb: [Bob Worgul] travesty of proverb by spoonerism, curtailment, portmanteau, what happens when you "mix a maxim": "All roads gather no moss.", "All work and no play make jack.", "Time wounds all heels.", "Better never than late."
petede: ["primum ego, tum ego, deinde ego" acronym] first I, then I, thereafter I; me, myself and I
petitio principii: aka begging the question, assuming what is to be proven
petroglitch: [petroglyph + glitch portmanteau] miscarved rock carving
petrool: [petroleum + drool portmanteau] slow, seemingly endless strand of motor oil at the end of the can
pfalindrome: word that would be a palindrome if not for the second letter: barb, blob

phalindrome: [Luc Étienne, phonetic palindrome portmanteau] word pronounced the same backward as forward, but not spelled the same (without b, hard c, d, hard g, k, p, t and only some l, m, n, r and y): babe, dude, known, mime, rare

phananyms: [phonetic ananym, proto-Tibetan] words that are ananyms phonetically, though not literally: fleshpot = top-shelf, nowhere = Erewhon (Samuel Butler), oat = toe, scoops = spooks,

phantonym pie: to scramble as in an anagram, a Denby Dale pie [Peter Newby] is the largest word made from edible words: dried peas + salt + onion + meat + fat = departmentalisations

phantasmogorishable: like pandigital pseudonumeral of phantasmagorishable (8210374695)

phemism: [dys/euphemism back-formation] between "bad" dysphemism and "good" euphemism

pheph: ["Post hoc ergo propter hoc" fallacy acronym] after this therefore because of this

pheresis: [beheaded apheresis] bigrammic beheadment

phhi: [pi : phi :: phi : ?] $\phi^{2\pi}$ = 0.833346100...

Phidias' Law: "61.8% of everything is the golden ratio."

phie: phi's and e's digits alternating, 1.267118802383198...

philirenic: peace-loving

phyllistine: [philistine mondegreen] like Phyllis Stein, artistic, cultured, well-educated

phinary: [2 : phi :: binary : ?] referring to ambiguous number system based on phi, ϕ, the golden ratio

phi-osophy: [phi + philosophy portmanteau] the study of the beauty and truth in the golden ratio, ϕ

phalindrome: [phonetic palindrome portmanteau] word that sounds the same backward and forward: babe, known

phatlu: [acronym] "People hate, as the love, unreasonably."

pheph: ["Post hoc ergo propter hoc." acronym] if-then fallacy

pho: [fi : fie : fo :: phi : phie : ?] $phie^{2/\phi}$ = 0.99230922...

phobograph: photograph of Phobos, the moon of Mars

pholynyms: [polynyms + h] words except for an extra second letter are like ones with two or more of the characteristics of allonym, ambinym, ananym, anatonym, antonym, apostronym, aptronym, arithmonym, boustrophenym, capitonym, consonym, contronym, domunym, exonym, euonym, feminyms, grammanym, heteronym, homonym, iatronym, liponym, malonym, meronym, morsonym, ouijanym, pianonym, retronym, roonym, synonym, tautonym, telephonym, toonym

phomeal: looped homealp, alphabetical anagram with last five letters moved to head

phorgetphul: unable to remember when to spell with an f or a ph

phum: [fi : fie : fo : fum :: phi : phie : pho : ?] $pho^{2/phie}$ = $phie^{3/\phi}$ = 1.2573368...

pi-prime: prime that is rounded multiple of pi, 3, 31, 314159

pianc: [Pecuniain arbotis non crescit.] Money doesn't grow on trees.

pianiog: [Disraeli acronym] "Patience is a necessary ingredient of genius."

pianonym: word limited to piano key letters, A, B, C, D, E, F or G: acceded, aged, baggage, bead-edged, begged, cabbage, gaged, dad, defaced, effaced, face, gab, gag,

pianonum: number in hexadecimal limited to piano key letters, A, B, C, D, E, F or G

pie: pi's and e's digits alternating, 3.271148125891...

piep: [Purgamentun init, exit purgamentum] Garbage in, garbage out

Pierson's Law: If you're coasting, you're going downhill.

Pig Latin homonym: word ending in the phoneme -(w)ā that means something else translated into English: airway (ware, wear, where), anyway (any), ashtray (trash), assay (sass), away (a), obey (beau, bow), olé (lo), outlay (lout), unsay (sun)

pig-headed: [pigheaded hyphenym] describing a word beginning with pig- but not referring to pigs: pigeon, pigment, pigmy

pigmint: [pigment mondegreen] breath freshener for swine

pile-it: [pilot mondegreen] what you do after cutting and splitting wood

pilck: [in a pick L wordle] in a bad situation

pillfer: [pilfer + pill portmanteau] steal prescription drugs

pin-headed: [pinhead hyphenym] describing a word beginning with pin- but not referring to pin: pince-nez, pincer, pinch-hit, pinchpenny, pine, pineapple, ping, pinion, pink, pinkie, pinnacle, pinniped, pinochle, pint

Pineapple Principle -- "The best parts of anything are inseparable from its worst."

pingle: [paleologism] struggle, strive; play with food; small enclosed field; long-handled cooking pot

pins: [Herbert acronym] "Poverty is no sin."

pint-sized: four-lettered

pipe down: [mondegreen] remove pipe from pipe organ to speak rather smoke, see pipe up

pipe organ: [mondegreen] mouth with which one smokes a pipe

pipe up: [pipe down antonym] move pipe back up to pipe organ to smoke rather than speak

pit: [pacem in Terra] peace on Earth

pitaoh: [Vauvenargues acronym] "Patient is the art of hoping."

pitch camp: [mondegren] promote unconventionality for the sake of humor

pitdib: [Robert Gilfillan acronym] "Poetry is truth dwelling in beauty."

pith helmet: [pithy back-formation] legendary headgear that endows the wearer with brevity, clarity and substance, analogous to thinking cap

pitvof: [Richard Henry Horne acronym] "Prayer is the voice of faith."

pitycoat: [petticoat mondegreen] old, somewhat shabby, but well-loved, coat, particularly Columbo-like trenchcoat

piyan: ["Plus If You Act Now" acronym] miscellaneous item piled on as a telemarketing ploy

pladd: [plaid + add portmanteau] add plaid to what one is already wearing

pleonasm: redundant or superfluous word(s)

plipogram: [palindronic lipogram portmanteau] passage both lipogrammic and palindromic

plaemoh: [homealp ananym] zeewyexical anagram with first four letters moved to tail

Plato-Socrates paradox: two statements which refer to each other which cannot both be true

play-dough: counterfeit money, currency used in a game

poacher: [mondegreen] someone who prefers to cook their eggs poached rather than sunny-side-up, scrambled or otherwise

plooing: [looped "loop"] anagram formed by moving the final letter to the initial position

plumage: [plus + mage portmanteau] superior wizard

plutoe: [plus + toe portmanteau] big toe

plutonic: [plus + tonic portmanteau] superior elixir

pnumerology: variant numerology which transforms words into palindromic numbers

po: [Tom Graves] answer to question not answerable with simple yes or no

poar: ["Paupertas omnium artium repertrix." acronym] Poverty [is the] inventor of all the arts; necessity is the mother of invention

pocketwatch: [pocket watch mondegreen] look-out for pickpockets while out in public
poèm trouvé: [Fren. "found poem] prose text reorganized to emphasize the poetry
poggly: any improbable construct that furthers speculation
pointless: without radix point, as in Bab. number system or cisfinite numbers
polar eyes: [polarize mondegreen] adaption that protects against snow blindness
polly-no-meal: [polynomial mondegreen] overfed parrot needing to cut back
polyalphabetical: [having interwoven alphabetical sequences: the bialphabetic "femininity" = emnn + fiiity = fmnn + eiiity
polygram: set of letters: bigram, trigram, …
polynyms: words with two or more of the characteristics of allonym, ambinym, ananym, anatonym, antonym, apostronym, aptronym, arithmonym, boustrophenym, capitonym, consonym, contronym, domunym, exonym, euonym, feminyms, grammanym, heteronym, hiddenym, homonym, iatronym, liponym, malonym, meronym, morsonym, mynynym, omonym, ouijanym, pianonym, postronym, retronym, roonym, synonym, tautonym, telephonym, toonym
polyphonic: describes transformation of letters into numbers and v. v. differently from pseudnumerology septemvigintary or telephonum, 0 = space, 1 = ADPY, 2 = BENZ, 3 = CMX, 4 = FKTW, 5 = GS, 6 = HU, 7 = ILV, 8 = JOQR: polyphonic = 1,871,168,273
polysemy: multiple meanings for words spelled the same
polysingular: refers to words with same plural but different singular forms: axes (ax, axis), bases (base, basis)
polythink: [2 : n :: doublethink : ?] to hold many thoughts, particularly contradictory ones, simultaneously
pombudsman: [pomegranate + buds + man portmanteau ≈ ombudsman] person who tends flowering pomegranate tree
pontisti: [Italian] experts at scheduling an unofficial holiday between the weekend and an official holiday, like Black Friday, the day after Thanksgiving
pooled: [loop ananym] looped and then reversed, for numbers the operation
poolnu: [unloop ananym] word unlooped and then reversed: flatcar = fractal
poortrait: [poor + portrait portmanteau] caricature and not a very good one
popigke: [pig in poke wordle] purchase made aziz with minimal information
poppysmic: [Lat. poppysyma] referring to lip-smacking
pornithology: [pornography + ornithology portmanteau] study of abnormal bird mating habits
porpoiseful: [porpoise + purposeful portmanteau] with the determination of a dolphin
porridginal: [porridge + original portmanteau] describing undiluted oatmeal
portmanteau: [Lewis Carroll] conflation of two words: chuckle + snortle = chortle, slanted + perpendicular = slantindicular, smoke + fog = smog; [James Joyces] bungelars, heliotrollops, murmoirs, perhelps …
poshlost: [Vladimir Nabokov] cliché-ridden, corny, crude, dishonest, moronic, trashy or vulgar
post hoc: ["post hoc, ergo propter hoc"] fallacy of mistaking primacy for causality
post-trophy: [apostrophy mondegreen] award given after recipient's death
postgenitor: [progenitor antonym] descendant
posthunanimous: [posthumous + unanimous portmanteau] unwilling to compromise even unto martyrdom
postMark: [capitonym] after break-up with Mark
postronym: [apostronym back-formation] word which becomes another word with apostrophe added: cant, ill, hell, shell, well

postsemi: [Dmitri Bergmann's last-half word] word with only letters after m: nonsupport, not, or, poppy, support, tro, two, wotro, wunty, zoo

potatot: [potato + tot portmanteau] small, bite-sized potato tuber

potlatch: [Haida] giving away of material wealth, even competitive generosity, to improve social status, detachment, community

Potter's Law: The amount of flak over any subject varies inversely to its value.

Poulsen's Law: When anything's used to its full potential (aka breaking point), it'll break. (See Schmidt's Law)

Poulter's glerint: [Anglo-Ferengi] Poulter's gross squared, seven-to-the-twelfth, $14^6 = 7^{12} = 13,841,287,201$

Poulter's gross: [dozen : Poulter's dozen :: gross : ?] fourteen cubed, seven-to-the-sixth, $14^3 = 7^6 = 117,649$

poultry reading: [poetry reading mondegreen] reading poetry to hens in order to increase egg production

pourous: [porous mondegreen] abole to be poured, liquid

powerless: [powerful back-formation] not divisible by a prime square, Πp_i^n, $n < 2$

powerful: divisible by a prime squared, $p^2 q$

power tower: aka high stacks, series of exponentiations from being expressed as superscriptions

prankuary: [prank + sanctuary portmanteau] refuge from practical jokes and tricksters

praying mantra: [preying mantis mondegreen] repetitive chant used in worship

pre-amble: [preamble hyphenym] preparation for a walk

pre-cent: [present mondegreen] ha'penny

pre-date: [predate hyphenym] preparations so that a social engagement can be arranged

pre-destined: [predestine hyphenym] prepared to get off at a pre-planned destination

pre-disposed: [predisposed hyphenym] describes trash put out before the pick-up time

pre-face: [preface mondegreen] whatever might come out of one's nose or mouth

pre-fur: [prefer mondegren] hairless, as of a newborn marsupial

pre-pear: [prepare mondegreen] between pear blossom and fruit

pre-perp: [mynynym] potential criminal

presemi: [Dmitri Bergmann's first-half of alphabet) word] word with only letters before n, like like, fiddle-faddle, see postsemi

pressedidigitation: [pressed + prestidigitation portmanteau] "magically" remembering how to decipher Roman numerals, as when asked the year a movie was made

pressured cooker: [pressure cooker mondegreen] one who is under stress as short-order or cook-off cook

prewed: [prude back-formation] made more scrupulous, more easily offended

Price's Law: If everyone doesn't want it, no one gets it.

primemate: [primate mondegreen] composite number companion to a prime number by substituting 0, 1, 2, 3, 4 for 9, 8, 7, 6, 5 and v. v.

prime: number with no factors except one and itself

prime density: prime per total numbers in sequence

prime twins: primes with common neighbor

primee: [prime + preemie] prime number enthusiast

primeval: [Mike Keith] able to form more primes with same digits, like 13 and 31

printrovert: [print introvert portmanteau] person who prefers the company of books to people

private delective: [private detective mondgreen] secret pleasure

private eye: [mondegreen] eye hidden behind eyepatch or dark sunglasses
private investigator: someone who investigates privates whether within or outside the army
pro toe-type: [prototype mondegreen] type with one's toe like a professional
pro-cord: [concord antonym] describes grapes
pro-dorp: [mynynym] in favor of small towns and villages
pro-liftic: [prolific + lift portmanteau] able to lift weights many times in a row
pro-noun: [pronoun hyphenym] person, place or thing that has lost its amateur status
pro-pain: [propane mondegreen] believing that physical suffering can be spiritually redemptive
pro-teen: [protein mondegreen] supportive of young people between twelve and twenty
pro-tractor: [protractor hyphenym] supporting farm equipment
problem-size effect: difficulty in solving a problem varies with the complexity of the mathematics but also with the numbers and transcoding and reformulating involved
proct: [proctor back-formation] monitor test-taking students
proem: [prose poem portmanteau] aka poème trouvé, prose that reads like poetry: [Dr. William Whewell] "There is no force, however great, can stretch a cord, however fine, into a horizontal line, which is accurately straight."
professed: [prof- mondegreen] describes word beginning with prof- that generates a fictitious name: Prof. Fess, Prof. Fitz
profetti: [confetti antonym] small pieces of color paper used to celebrate a prophet or his/her prophesies
promythium: moral at beginning of fable
pronundrum: [conundrum antonym] punning question that goes with straight-sounding answer, ala Carnac the Magnificent
propa ganda: [proper gander mondegreen] male goose when courting, before becoming papa gander
prosthesis: addition of letter or syllable to word: "irregardless"
prototypical: [George Lakoff] between one and nine, $1 \leq n \leq 9$
proxy mate: [approximate mondegren] substitute companion, the one you're with rather than the one you would rather be with
pryme: nymber which is prime both as an arithmonym and in septemgesimal
psa: ["puri sermonis amator" acronym] lover of pure speech
psem: ["Proximus sum egomet mihi." acronym] I am closest to myself
pseudo-antonym: word or phrase that seems to be an antonym for another but is not: catwalk vs. dogtrot, cold feet vs. hot heads, maternity dress vs. paternity suit, overlay vs. understand
pseudo-comparitive: word that ends in -er that is not a comparative, see pseudo-superlative: beer, temper,
pseudoliterature: Freudianist, racist or classist propaganda
pseudo-superlative: word that ends in -est that is not a superlative, see pseudo-comparitive: pest, tempest
pseudo-synonym: word or phrase that sound like the meaning of another but is not: air force vs. windpower, central time vs. middle ages, high command vs. tall order, raindrop vs. waterfall
pseudonum: word's number in pseudonumerology
pseudonumeral: number's pseudonym in pseudonumerology

pseudonumerology: [Allen Krill] fka memory dynamics [William Fauver] and phrenomnemotechny [Francis Fauvel-Gouraud] study of phonetic numbers
pseudovampire: vampire except for terminating zeroes
pshiftgrams: words that are both palindromes and shiftgrams, eye/gag, dud/ere
psychobabble: psychological doubletalk
psychophant: [psychopath + sychopant portmanteau] servant who could turn on you at any time
psychophonic: having to do with precognitive awareness of a telephone's ringing
Pudder's Law: Anything that begins well ends badly. Anything that begins badly ends worse.
pukka: [paleologism] reliable information, see duff
pully: [pulley mondegreen] tugging again and again on something or someone as a young child on its mother's leg
pumectation: [Harry Matthews] hiding the underlining structure of a work
pun gent: [pungent charade] gentleman punster
pundarika: [Sanskrit] ten-to-the-hundred-twelfth, hundred-twelveplex, 10^{112}
pundrome: [punning palindrome portmanteau] phalind(d)romic sentence: "Find bee or be fined!", "Knight, buy Whale's Inn wine or whine in Wales by night.", "Mary, maid missed in mist, made merry!", "No eye sees the seas I know."
punnishment: [pun + punishment portmanteau] inflicting wordplay on listeners
punslinger: [pun + gunslinger portmanteau] expert punster
pupuddle: [pup + puddle portmanteau] what puppy makes before being house trained
pure: describes words with letters from a particular section of the alphabet, see inword, innerword, innestword, mid-word, midderword, middererword, middestword, outword, outerword, outestword
pure math: [G. H. Hardy] beautiful but useless, see num
purebread: [purebred mondegreen] what organic whole wheat toast is made from
Puritan's Law: Evil is live spelled backwards.
purple: ornate with striking imagery, lively detail
purspiration: [purse + perspiration portmanteau] what collects on a handbag left out early in the morning
pushoffer: [push off back-formation ≈ pushover] someone who pushes another off rather than letting themselves becoming a pushover
puzzl: [curtailed puzzle] jigsaw puzzle missing the last piece or crossword puzzle missing the last word
pwnonum: [pwnonym + -number portmanteau] misprinted number
pwnonym: misprinted word
pyramid: word with letter frequencies of 1, 2, 3, 4, ...: beerbibber, isosmosis, keennesses, redefferred, rememberer, reremember, rereverses, sanenesses, sereneness, sleeveless, knelllessnesses, linenlessnesses
pyrosomniac: [pyromaniac + insomniac portmanteau] someone who smokes in bed
Q-graphable: [quadrature, Leonard Gordon] graphable as if on a quadratic tiling: hyperthyroidization
qaca: ["Quique amavit, cras amet." acronym] May he love tomorrow who's never loved before.
qah: ["Quo ad hoc." acronym] as much as this

qam: ["Quid agis, medice?" acronym] What's up, Doc?

qapaerf: ["Quidquid agis, prudenter agas et respice finem!" acronym] Whatever you do, do cautiously, and look to the end.

qed: ["quod erat demonstratrandum." acronym] that which was to be demonstrated

qic: ["Quod incepimus conficiemus." acronym] What we've begun we'll finish.

qintmocag: [Samuel Johnson acronym] "Questioning is not the mode of conversation among gentlemen."

qop run: [Peter Newby] trigram like "qop" made up of three consequative letters: ABC, bac, cab, dec, ghi, mon, nom

quackamoo: [duck's quack + cow's moo] duck-billed, cow-faced creature, possibly a hadosaur

quadisograms: four words with no letters in common: gadfly, punchworks, vext, zimb

quadralphabetical: describes word not able to be separated into just three alphabetical sequences: like alphabetical = alpt + hil + abc + a

quadruplet: [triplet extrapolation] changing one word to another three letters at a time

quadwrangle: [quad + wrangle ≈ quadrangle] intermural competition between the four dormitories

quarterback: twenty-five percent refund

quartersibling: half-sibling's half-sibling

quash: [beheaded squash] quell, crush

quasi: describes anything with quasiness, a distortion from the truly Real, the real-unreal striving for real realness.

quasi-antonym: word or phrase that looks like an antonym but isn't: burn down (burn-up), fat chance (slim chance), irregardless (regardless), loosen (unloosen)

quatch: [paleologism] sound; pudgy

quaternade: word whose every fourth letter is four smaller words: pantaloonery = pan + ale + nor + toy

quatrain: 4 verses rhyming abab

quattordicina: poem with $14^2 = 196$ lines

quattrina: [George Pierce] poem with 16 lines rhyming $4! = 24$ ways

qubit: multivalued quantum bit

quelch: [beheaded squelch] suppress, crush

Quenelejeff's table: [Queneau + Medelejeff portanteau, *Atlas delittérature potentielle*] table categorizing 56 kinds of linguistic operands by 8 operations

	displacement	substitution	addition	subtraction	multiplication	division	deduction	contraction
letter	Ia	IIa	IIIa	IVa	Va	VIa	VIIa	VIIIa
phoneme	Ib	IIb	IIIb	IVb	Vb	VIb	VIIb	VIIIb
syllable	Ic	IIc	IIIc	IVc	Vc	VIc	VIIc	VIIIc
word	Id	IId	IIId	IVd	Vd	VId	VIId	VIIId
syntagm	Ie	IIe	IIIe	IVe	Ve	VIe	VIIe	VIIIe
sentence	If	IIf	IIIf	IVf	Vf	VIf	VIIf	VIIIf
paragraph	Ig	IIg	IIIg	IVg	Vg	VIg	VIIg	VIIIg

quenina: [*Subsidia Pataphysica* by Raymond Queneau] poem with a number of verses suitable for spirally permuting like the sestina in Queneau's numbers = (p - 1)/2: 5, 9 (nonina), 11 (undicina), 14 (quattordicina), 18 (diciottina), 23, 26, 29,30, 33, 35, 39, 41, ... verses

quetch: [paleologism] twitch; break silence

quick-change: telephonym with each telephonum different from the previous one: electroencephalography = 3532876362374256472749

quid pro quo pro: professional practitioner of the Golden Rule

quinade: word which every fifth letter forms five smaller words: paramelaconites = pen + ali + rat + ace + mos

quincuncial: number system based on both five and twelve like Selelvians

quindicina: poem with $15^2 = 225$ lines

quintain: 5-line poem

quintisograms: five words with no letters in common: chintz, fjord, gawky, plumbs, vex

quintuplet: [quadruplet extrapolation] changing one word into another four letters at a time

quizl: [quiz + puzzle] near word with different final letter(s), not a portmanteau as would be "quizzle" or a mere paragram as would be "puzzl"

qwaint: [O. E. qwaint] word-like letter-sequence possessing the quality of the word suggested: ampers&, caMel, Decembrrr, defectiv, dynamight, exc!amation, fffreezing, inelastick, lithp, mispelling, neverendin, psighchoanalysis, slowth, twogether, vwlss

R-graphable: [rookwise, Leonard Gordon] graphable as if moving rookwise-laryngopharyngectomies

r-invariant: describes words with r only in the 18th place: hemidemisemiquaver, psychogalvanometer, thermoelectrometer

raa: ["reductio ad absurdum" acronym] reduction to the absurd, proving the truth of a proposition by proving the falsity of all its alternatives

rabdology: [John Napier] use of rods, such as Napier's, for calculating

radish: [mondegreen] somewhat radical

Ragari: describes words which change to another word when a double vowel with an r between is reduced to the vowel: Arab (ab), iris (is), riding (ring), riling (ring), thorough (tough), tiring (ting), wiring (wing), see Af Jinni

rained out: [mondegreen] describes a rain cloud that has emptied itself of its rain and is just a partly cloud

rainbowtie: [rainbow + bowtie portmanteau] festive multicolored neckwear

raios: ["Risus abundat in ore stultorum." acronym] Laughs are abundant in the mouth of the foolish.

rajatqoal: [acronym] "Reason and judgment are the qualities of a leader."

ralflagly: [rally around flag wordle] behave patriotically

ralucric:[circular ananym] describing words that are readable clockwise and counterclockwise when written circularly

randumb: [random + dumb portmanteau] not-quite truly random

rankor: [rank + rancor portmanteau] bitterness over malodorous stink

ransposition; [beheaded transposition] transformation of word by combined transposition and deletion: sonnet = notes + n = steno + n = stone + n = tones + n = nonet + s = tonne + s = nones + t, see aagram, angram, nagram,

ransposition string: string formed by ransposing: sonnetonestenonestone = sonnet + tones + steno + nones + stone

rare: refers to words with rare letters (j = 8, q = 10, x = 8, z = 10 scrabble pts.)

rash: [beheaded brash, trash] acting hastily and unwisely, critically or unprofitably

Rashomon effect: [the film "Rashomon"] the effect on a story of telling it from multiple points of view

Raspberry Jam Law: The wider any culture is spread, the thinner it gets.

rather large: [Joseph S. Madachy] as high or higher than to-the-fourth-nine $\geq {}^4 9$

ratiocinitis: [A. K. Dewdney] tendency to abuse numerator or denominator in ratio or percentage

Rawson's First Law: As soon as you dispose of a book, a pressing need to refer to it will arise.

Re: [Percy Er] doubly curtailed, reversed, then triply curtailed and reversed again

re-incarnation: [reincarnation hypenym] pouring unused condensed milk back into the can

re-leaf: [relief mondegreen] what trees do ever spring

re-leveler: [mynynym] one who levels again

re-pose: [repose hyphenym] what an artist's model often does standing, sitting and/or reclining

re-treat: [retreat hyphenym] take yet another sweet

rean: [Eccl 7:16] "Righteousness exalteth a nation."

rebru number: [number palindrome] aka numberdrome or emordnilap number that reads the same forward and backward

rebus: pictorial or symbolic communication: [Louis XV] P/Venez a 6/100 = Venez sous P, a cent sous six = Venez souper a Sans Souci, [Voltaire]Ga = G grand, a petit = J'ai grand app,tit = I'm hungry, fault(b/(husband(quarrel)wife))fault = Be above a quarrel between a husband and a wife; there are faults on both sides., "If the B mt put :but if the B . putting :" = If the grate be empty put coal on but if the grate be full stop putting coal on., stand/I take/U 2/throw taking/my = I understand you undertake to overthrow my undertaking., IVNKT: "IVIMKT. FUNEX?" "SVFXKT.""FUNEM?" "SVFM2." "OKILFDMNX." "CKTDMNX!" "GGGARNOMNX!" "SAR2XKT.CMXMNXXNM?" "OIC! ICDX. ICDM. ICDXRNDMNDMNDX. YYURYYIV. ICIVVVYY4KT." = Ivy, I em Katie. 'Ave you any eggs? 'Es, ve 'ave eggs, Katie. 'Ave you any 'em? 'Es, ve 'ave 'em too. Okay, I'll 'ave de 'em 'n' eggs. See, Katie, the 'em 'n' eggs! Jeez, 'ey aren' no 'em 'n' eggs. 'Es, 'ey are too 'em 'n' eggs, Katie. See, 'em, eggs, 'em 'n' eggs, eggs 'n' 'em?. O, I see de eggs! I see de 'em. I see de eggs are in de 'em 'n' de 'em in de eggs. Too wise you are, too wise, Ivy. I see Ivy's too wise for Katie.,stand/I take/U 2/throw taking/my = I understand you undertake to overthrow my undertaking., L/AF/D = A F on D L over (a fond lover),we-shall/come = We shall overcome.

reciprocal automynocagram: [J. A. Lindon] two passages whose acronyms are each other: "Some thoughtful and really intelligent new guests of Vera's entered ..." and "Staring over my empty top hat, Olga's uncle grimaced ..."

red-headed: [redheaded hyphenyn] describing a word beginning with red- but not referring to red: redact, redecorate, redeem, redeliver, redemption, redeploy, redesign, redevelop, redirect, redistribute, redistrict, redo, redolent, redress, reduce, reduction, redundant, reduplicate, redux

redew: [redo mondgreen] what the cool air does after the warm sunshine undewed the day before

redundancy: repeated word or phrase for emphasis: "and plus", "find and dandy", Manual dexterity", "old geezer", "over-exaggerate", "the truth, the whole truth and nothing but the truth", "unexpected surprise"

reduplicate: word with similar, even identical, frags: abracadabra, ack-ack, blackjack, bonbon, boogie-woogie, boohoo, bowwow, bye-bye, cancan, chiff chaff, chitchat, claptrap, click clack, creepy-crawly, dillydally, dingdong, drip-drop, fancy-pantsy, fiddle-faddle, flimflam, flipflop, gewgaw, goody-goody, handy-pandy, hanky-panky, harum-scarum, heebie-jeebies, helter skelter, higgeldy-piggeldy, hippety-hoppety, hocus-pocus, hokey pokey, hodgepodge, hoity-toity, hokey-pokey, holus-bolus, honky-tonk, hotsy-totsy, hurdy-gurdy, hurly-burly, jimjams, knickknack, lovey-dovey, mishmash, mumbo jumbo, namby-pamby, niddy-noddy, niminy-piminy, nitwit, nosy posy, okey dokey, pellmell, pish tush, pitpat, plitter-patter, pooh-pooh, ragtag, randem-tandem, randy-dandy, razzle-dazzle, ribble-rabble, riffraff, roly-poly, rusty-crusty, rustyfusty, seesaw, shilly-shally, slimslam, slipslop, snick snack, snipsnap, squish squash, super-duper, ta-ta, teeny tiny, teeny-weeny, tick-tock, tickle-tackle, tiptop, tisty tosty, tittle-tattle, topsy-turvy, tut-tut, walky-talky, whippersnapper, wibble-wobble, wiggle-waggle, willy-nilly, wishy-washy, zigzag or simply "something schmomething"

reeb: [beer ananym] reverse of fifty-five squared, five thousand two hundred three, 5,203

reen: [blue : bleen :: red : ?] red that turns green, like traffic light

regna: [Jap.] poem or number with $20(5 + 7 + 5 + 2(7)) = 620$ syllables

regular: not irregular, not dividing Bernoulli numerator

re-lax: [relax hyphenym] become unrigid again

rellow: [red + yellow portmanteau] red that changes to yellow like a traffic light

remini-scents: [reminiscents hyphenym] smell that triggers nosetalgia

Rep: [Percy Per] reversed, doubly curtailed and then reversed again

repdigit: with repeated digit, see monochromatic

Research Law: Enough research'll support a hypothesis; more than enough won't.

Researchers' Law: The probability of finding the source you need is inversely proportional to the distance to the source.

resisting a rest: [resisting arrest mondegreen] refusing to take a nap during nap time

restaurantese: jargon used in restaurants: chocker hole (donut), hounds (hot dogs), murk (coffee), whistleberries (beans)

retrocarbonation: malfunction of drink machine that dispenses the soda and then the cup

retronym: back-formation necessitated by innovation: acoustical vs. electric guitar

returnical: [return + rhetorical portmanteau] describing when waiters and waitresses wait until the customer's mouth is full before returning and asking the unanswerable question, "How is everything?"

revered: [rev- mondegreen] describes word beginning with rev- that generates a fictitious name: Rev. Ealer, Rev. Eller, Rev. Enger, Rev. Ert, Rev. Iser, Rev. Iving, Rev. Olting

Revelation Law: "The hidden flaw never remains hidden."

rhating: [hat in ring wordle] made bid for political office

rhope: [rope homonym, rhopalon, "club"] aka snowball, words which grow one letter or syllable: but, butt, butte, butter, buttery; melting snowball = antirhope

rhopalic: describes sentence that grows one letter per word: ["Liminal Poem" by Harry Mathews] "O to see man's stern poetic thought publicly espousing recklessly imaginative mathematical inventiveness, openmindedness unconditionally superfecundating, nonantagonistically hypersophisticated interdenominational.", "I am not here every single morning, moreover, yesterday unexpected, unwished-for catastrophic circumstances, unalteringly interfering, superseded initially hoped-for fragile dreams, alone down low am I."

rhotic: describes word whose r changed to a w: rabbit (wabbit), rack (whack), ram (wham), rascally (wascally), ray (way)

rhymed ring string: word string which turns back on itself compressed into a string: agag, anther, aper, are, aspas

riblo: [D'ni] to-the-second-twenty-five, $^225 = 25^{25} = 5^{50}$ = no-so-little fiftyplex, 88,817,841,970,012,523,233,890,533,447,265,625

rilen: [D'ni] twenty-five-to-the-twenty-third, $25^{23} = 5^{46}$ = not-so-little forty-sixplex, 142,108,547,152,020,037,174,224,853,515,625

rime couéé: tail rhyme, aaabcccb

rime léonine: 2-syllable rhyme

rime pauvre: [poor rhyme] with only vowel rhymed

rime riche: [rich rhyme] with whole syllable rhymed, consonants before and after and vowel

rime royal: [royal rhyme] 7 verses in iambic pentameter rhyming $(ab)^2bc^2$

rime suffisante: with final vowel and consonant

rimel: [D'ni] twenty-five-to-the-twenty-fourth, not-so-little forty-eightplex, $25^{24} = 5^{48}$ = 3,552,713,678,800,500,929,355,621,337,890,625

rira: [D'na] twenty-five-to-the-twenty-first, not-so-little forty-twoplex, $25^{21} = 5^{42}$ = 227,373,675,443,232,059,478,759,765,625

riš: [D'ni] twenty-five-to-the-twenty-second, not-so-little forty-fourplex, $25^{22} = 5^{44}$ = 5,684,341,886,080,801,486,968,994,140,625

rite of whey: [right of way mondegreen] cheese-making tradition

ritmaqoat: [Cicero acronym] "Reason is the mistress and queen of all things."

Ro: [Manx Roo] triply curtailed, reversed, then doubly curtailed

roaring: intimidatingly long, obscure or even nonce word: Samuel Johnson's "Woman, thou art a parallelogram!"

Rockmanese: [Flash Gordon] phonetically reversed word(s): arts (star), babe, but (tub), eat (tea), known

rodiamondugh: [diamond in rough wordle] unfinished masterpiece

rollercoaster: describes a word without all alphabetical, all zexical or any double letters: ado, after, cars, does, each, market, mist, pal, where

romantic: describing number with a Roman numeral in number name, such as fIVe, sIX, seVen, eIght, nIne, eLeVen, tweLVe, thIrteen, ...

Romanum: Roman numeral wordnum: I = 9, II = 18, III = 27, IV = 32, V = 23

romanym: [Roman + -nym] word with only Roman numeral letters (c, d, i, l, m, v, x): civic, civil, did, dim, id, lid, livid, mid, mild, millim, mimic, minim, mix, vim

romec: [Radix omnium malorum est cupiditas.] Love of money's the root of all evil.

Romwhene: [when in Rome wordle] call to conformity

rondeau: 13 to 20 verses with 2 rhymes and refrain

rondel: 13 to 14 verses with 2 rhymes and refrain

rondelet: [Fren.] poem or number with 2(4) + 2(8) or 4(8) + 4 = 24 syllables

Roo: [Manx Room] triply curtailed, reversed then curtailed again

roofest: [roof back-formation] roof that has been re-roofed again by a re-roofer

Room: [Percy Moor] triply curtailed and then reversed

roonum: number name with at least one other hidden inside, not related etymologically: twenty-one (two)

roonym: [kangaroo word] aka kangaroodle, marsupial word, word with at least one other word hidden inside, related in meaning to the larger, but not etymologically: barricade (bar), calumnies (lies), catacombs (tombs), container (can), chocolate (cocoa), clue (cue), contaminated (tainted), curtail (cut), deceased (dead), destruction (ruin), encourage (urge), exist (is), facade (face), illuminated (lit), instructor (tutor), latest (last), market (mart), masculine (male), matches (mates), observe (see), partially (partly), perambulate (amble), pinioned (pinned), postures (poses), prosecute (sue), rampage (rage), rapscallion (rascal), recline (lie), regulate (rule), respite (rest), rotund (round), slithered (slid), transgression (sin), unanimity (unity), utilise (use), see joey

roosting: first order nesting about base, $g(n, n', n'', n''') = g(n -1, n', n'', g(n', n'', n'''))$

rootbeer: [restaurantese] fifty-five, 55

Rothbard's Law: Everyone specializes in their area of weakness.

roundel: poem with 11 verses rhyming $abac(ab)^3c$

rounding error: rounding up rather than down, especially common with 5, see overrounding

roundness: number of prime factors relative to near neighbors

rubbee: [rubber back-formation] whatever rubber rubbs

rubbish: [rubber + -ish] somewhat like old rubber tires

rubugg: [bug in rug wordle] comfortable

ruck: [rucksack back-formation] contents of a rucksack

Rudin's Law: In crises, most people will choose the worst possible course of action.

RUMT: [grammanym] Are you empty?

Runamok's Law: There are four kinds of people: (a) those who sit quietly and do nothing, (b) those who talk about sitting quietly and doing nothing, (c) those who do things, and (d) those who talk about doing things.

Runyon's Law: [Damon Runyon] The race is not always to the swift, nor the battle to the strong, but that's the higher probability.

Ryan's Law: "Three consecutive correct guesses establishes you as an expert."

s-invariant: describes word with s only in the 19th place: agammaglobulinemias, angiocardiograhies, antirevolutionaries, encephalomeningitis, meningoencephalitis

s-lipogram: text without the letter S: "Hymn to Ceres and the Centaurs" by Lasus

s'urname: [apostronymous surname] surname beginning with s- turned to possessive with first name: Loretta's wit, Robert's tack

sa: [Talcryl] three in unit's place, otherwise four, in base seven; or [Sino-Korean] four

sabermetrics: baseball mathematics

sabsung: [Thai] quenching an emotional or spiritual thirst and the feeling after having an inexpressible need met

sacranym: [st- mondegreen] word beginning with st- that generates a fictitious name, like St. Able, St. Aid, St. Eady, St., Ern, St. Iff, St. Ingy, St. Ocky, St. Ogy, St. Oic, St. Olid, St. Ony, St. Out, St. Ray, St. Rict, St. Rong, St. Urdy

sacre: [curtailed sacred make something holy or [Fren. sacre blu] blue

saddle: something a horse or a person is burdened with whether they like it or not

safecracker: [mondegreen] thin bakery good that is found not to be poisonous

Sagan's fallacy: To say a human being is nothing but molecules is like saying a Shakespearean play is nothing but words.

Sagari: describes words which change to another word when a double vowel with an s between is reduced to the vowel: Isis (is), rising (ring), solo (so), whoso (who), see Af Jinni

sai: [Jap.] ten-to-the-forty-fourth, 10^{44}

samaptalambha: [Sanskrit] ten-to-the-thirty-ninth, 10^{39}

samudra: [Indian] ten-to-the-eighteenth, 10^{18}

sameallboat: [all in same boat wordle] together in a predicament

sangama: [Indian] ten-to-the-fourteenth, 10^{14}

sar: [Bab.] sixty-squared, $60^2 = 3,600$

sarchasm: [sarcasm + chasm portmanteau] gulf between sarcastic wit and the one who doesn't get it

sarges: [Bab.] sixty-cubed, 60^3 = 216,000

sarithmonym: [s- + arithmonym] word that becomes a number name if beheaded, like bone, cone, done, ...

saru: [gar : garu :: sar : ?] sixty-to-the-fourth, 60^4 = 12,960,000

sarvabala: [Sanskrit] ten-to-the-forty-seventh, 10^{47}

sarvajna: [Sanskrit] ten-to-the-fifty-first, 10^{54}

sasne: ["Sine ars scienta nihil est." acronym] Without art science is nothing.

sasqwatch: [sasquatch watch portmanteau] search for napes (N. American apes)

satisficing: [Herbert Simon] satisfactory and sufficient, but not the best

Sattinger's Law: It works better plugged in.

saurocide: [(dino)saur + -cide portmanteau] whatever it was that killed the dinosaurs

sbuttky: [buttinsky wordle] kibitzer

Schlimmbesserung: [German] so-called improvements that are nothing of the kind but make things worse, not quite the same as farpotshket

schmalindrome: word(s) that would be palindromic if not for the first four letters

schmanagram: word resulting from transaddition, adding four letters to and rearranging letters of original word

schmarithmonym: [schm- + arithmonym] word which becomes a number name if quadrupally beheaded: alone acetone, anemone, condone, cyclone, doggone, forgone, hipbone, ...

Schmidt's Law: If you mess with a thing long enough, it'll break. (See Poulsen's Law.)

schomonum: [sch- + homonum compound] number which becomes its own homonum when more than one leading zero is ignored

schpalindrome: word that would be a palindrome if initial three letters were deleted

scholar ship: [scholarship mondegreen] ocean-going vessel used for scientific exploration and instruction

Schuckit's Law: 100% of interference in human conduct has the potential for causing harm, no matter how innocuous.

schydration: [sch- + hydration portmanteau] adding three letters at the beginning of a word

sciancé: [science + fiancé portmanteau] science major about to be wedded to his profession

scoreteen: [rhymes with fourteen] twenty plus any teen, 36 ± 3

scorety: [rhymes with forty] twenty tens or two hundred, 200

Scott's Laws: (1) "The probability of something wrong looking right is greater than that of it looking wrong." (2) "When an error has been detected and corrected, it will be found to have been correct in the first place.

Scrabble sentence: sentence using all 100 Scrabble letters: "Countrymen, if I am to bury, not eulogize, Caesar, evil lives on, bequeathing injury, good expires a palsied, oft awkward, death!"

screwtinny: [screw + scrutiny portmanteau] especially close examination with virtual thumb screws

scriptible: [Roland Barthes] writerly, with meaning not immediately evident

scruple: [scruples back-formation] lone qualm, twinge of doubt or hesitation at a dilemma

sea: ["Scribere est agre." acronym] to write is to act.

sea son: [season mondegreen] boy born onboard a ship

Seay's Law: Nothing ever comes out as planned.

secondary: [elementary antonym] word with non-element letters, counting D and T as isotopes of H: A, D, E, G, J, L, M, Q, R, T, X, Z: aggregate, amalgamate, axe, dead, deeded, degree, delete, delegate, elated, exaggerate, extralegal, extreme, grade, greater, greed, jade, later, mate, Qatar, regret, trader, zeal
scent-he-meant: [sentiment mondegreen] perfume that the buyer should have bought as a gift, rather that the one he did
(**Seeger's Law**: Anything in parentheses can be ignored.)
Segal's Law: A man with a watch knows what time it is; a man with two's never sure.
sejant: [paleologism] sitting
sei: [Jap.] ten-to-the-fortieth, fortyplex, 10^{40}
selective attention: fallacy of paying more attention to confirming than contradictory evidence
self-control: mastery of one's own inner throttle
self-frighteous: [self-righteous + fright portmanteau] thinking so much on scary things sights and sounds it's scary
Sells' Law: The first sample is the best sample.
semihidden: hidden charade paired with an unhidden word: "No mad nomad would talk about a bout with a thinking, thin king.", "A lei sure adds to one's sense of leisure.", "car pet carpet", "The victim mumbled, stabbed, then mum, bled to death.", "How long will that dingo din go on!", "Look how fat her father is!", "There's poison in the poi, son.", "The chaplain asked had the injured chap laid long.", "Men sans Mensans are densans.", "The winds in Juneau gust in June-August." "If I begin to drink, my choice'll be gin."
semo-definitional: [Marcel Bénabou and Georges Perec] having had substituted definitions for words
semordnilap: ["palindromes" ananym] ananym pair
senatorial: [sen-/cen- mondegreen] describes word beginning with cen-/sen- that generates a fictitious name: Sen. Tennial, Sen. Ter, Sen. Sibyl, Sen. Tree
sensawunda: [sense of wonder] awe of natural wonders or BDOs
sensitivity: true-positive rate of test, see specificity, accuracy and background
sep: ["Sapientia est potentia." acronym] Knowledge is power.
septemvigintary: [Lee Sallows] system of transforming word(s) to numbers via base 27, with space = 0: so that: anti + bulk = diet, antics + reveal = stones, (at)x(king) =stove, (cram)x(zip) = corpses, cube + polo = tint, gauche + hairdo = occult, inch + mail = volt, (forty-two + forty-nine)(mod 6) = one, circle (mod love) = flag, hangs (mod green) = jibe
Septober: [September + October portmanteau] 61 days between August and November
septuplet: [sextuplet extrapolation] changing one word into another six letters at a time
sercon: [serious + constructive] constructive but not playful about it
seriohumorous: [cirrocumulus cloud ≈ serious + humorous portmanteau] describes clown that is both serious and humorous
Service's Law: It's later than you think.
servile: [serve + vile portmanteau] willing to assist an evil, mad scientist
sesquation: operation between addition and multiplication as with 0 + 0 = 0x0 = 0
sesquidecimal: base fifteen, n_{15}
sestet: poem with 6 lines rhyming a^3bab
sestina: [Swinburne] 6-stanza poem with 6-versed stanzas spirally permutated as if by shuffling end half between front half: 123456, 615243, 364125, 532614, 451362, 51362
settina: [George Perce] poem with $7^2 = 49$ lines in a spiral scheme rhyme

Sevareid's Law: "The chief cause of problems is solutions."
severe: describes a thunderstorm so noisy that it does not allow speaking in class
sextuplet: [quintuplet extrapolation] changing one word into another five letters at a time
sexy: separated by six in sequence, a number and its sixth successor
shadow box: [shadowbox charade] box that a mime may trap him/herself and/or his/her shadow in
shalindrome: word(s) that would be palindromic if not for the first two letters
shambulls: [shambles mondegreen] mechanical bulls that can be attempted to be ridden in a country-western bar
shammy: [chamois homonym] imitation chamois soft cloth
shanagram: word resulting from transaddition, adding two letters to and rearranging letters of original word
Shanahan's Law: A meeting's length is inversely proportional to the square of the number of attendees and its productivity inversely proportional to its length. (see Walinsky's Law)
shandygaff: beer diluted with a nonalcoholic drink
shanku: [Indian] ten-to-the-twelfth, twelveplex, 10^{12}
shetaordlu: [etaoin shrdlu wordle] more pronounceable version of 12 commonest letters
sheugh: [paleologism] ditch, trench
shiftwords: words which can be transformed into each other by round-the-horn alphabet shifts: abjurer + 13 = nowhere, adz + 5 = fie, ado + 5 = fit, air + 12 = mud, alohas + 6 = grungy, asp + 2 = cur, ass - 4 = woo, box + 3 = era, bra + 9 = sir, bug + 6 = ham, cheer + 7 = jolly, dud + 1 = ere, dye + 2 = fag, egg + 8 = moo, end + 1 = foe, errs + 13 = reef, eye + 2 = gag, fusion + 6 = layout, ice + 2 = keg, inkier + 7 = purply, lab + 3 = ode, lob + 3 = ore, manful + 7 = thumbs, not + 5 = sty, odd + 11 = zoo, ohm + 1 = pin, orb + 3 = rue, pry + 3 = sub, rye + 2 = tag, steeds + 1 = tuffet, sue + 6 = yak, yes - 10 = oui
shiftword chain: add +1 = bee + 7 = ill, ant + 11 = lye + 2 = nag, ape + 11 = lap + 4 = pet, ark + 3 = dun + 14 = rib, bed + 7 = ilk + 9 = rut, bin + 6 = hot + 7 = ova, don + 5 = its + 1 = jut, flap + 13 = sync + 6 = yeti, fur + 6 = lax + 7 = she, hep + 4 = lit + 7 = spa, irk + 9 = rat + 4 = vex, see collinear
shih: [Chinese] insightful, elegant knowledge marked by good taste and good judgment
shirsha prahelika purvi: eight-million-four-hundred-thousand-to-the-twenty-eighth, $8,400,000^{28} > 10^{169}$
shlop: [shirt + slop portmanteau] condition of a shirt that has been improperly buttoned
shmalindrome: word(s) that would be palindromic if not for the first three letters
shmanagram: word resulting from transaddition, adding three letters to and rearranging letters of original word
shpalindrome: word that would be a palindrome if initial two letters were deleted
shkickins: [kick in shins wordle] painful, though minor, wounding
shmarithmonym: [shm- + arithmonym] word which becomes a number name if triply beheaded: anyone, begone, bygone, debone, intone, ketone, redone, rezone, ...
shoebox: [mondegreen] kick box with one's shoes on
shomonym: word which becomes its own homonym when beheaded: aisle, Gnome, llama, knap, knave, kneed, knew, knickers, knight, knit, knot, hour, psalter, scent, whole, wrap, wrest, wretch, wright, write, wrote
shomonum: [sh- + homonum portmanteau] number which becomes its own homonum when a leading zero is ignored
shydration: [sh- + hydration portmanteau] adding two letters at the beginning of a word

sibi: [Sino-Korean, sip + i] twelve
sibil: [Sino-Korean, sip + il] eleven
sibo: [Sino-Korean, sip + o] fifteen
sibot: [South acronym] "Society is built on trust."
side division: dividing a number horizontally as those with one(s) and/or eight(s) into those with one(s) and zero(es)
sien: [Stultorum infinitus est numerus.] Infinite is the number of fools.
sighclops: [sigh + cyclops portmanteau] car with one headlight in danger of becoming a car with no headlights
sighted: [blind back-formation] refers to number name with at least one i: five, six, eight, nine
sigmagon: [sigma + -gon] stellated polygon formed from sigma-like quintuple line segments
sigmatic: describes words whose th phoneme changes to s, the opposite of lisping: thank (sank), thigh (sigh), thing (sing), think (sink), thump (sump)
silly similies: right as cramp [writer's cramp], full as earth [fuller's earth]
Silverson's Paradox: "If anything can go wrong with Murphy's Law, it will."
Simon's Law: Everything put together comes apart.
simpaticocoa: [simpatico + cocoa portmanteau] soothing, warm, shared hot chocolate
siok: [Spenser acronym] "Science is organized knowledge."
sip: [Sino-Korean] ten
siscaib: [T. H. Huxley acronym] "Science is simply common sense at its best."
sisi: [Summum ius summa inuria. acronym] The more law [there is] the less justice.
sithornde: [thorn in side wordle] seemingly incurable pain
sitcoe: [George Henry Lewes acronym] "Science is the systematic classification of experience.]
sitdot: [Chesterfield acronym] "Style is the dress of thoughts."
slenderize: remove a certain letter from the text to generate new text
slog: aka super-logarithm, number to which another number has been tetrated, n = $\text{slog}_{n'}$ ($^{n}n'$), $\text{slog}_n(0) = 1$, $\text{slog}_n(1) = 0$, see height
sloover: [soap slivver portmanteau] small remnant of soap useable only within washcloth
sloppage: [slop + slippage portmanreau] sloppy sandwich contents that slip out
slottery: [slot + lottery portmanteau] checking coin returns as if they were slot machines hoping to "win" a small winfall
slysocide: [slice + -ocide portmanteau] act of murdering a slice of bread with a knife and cold butter
small: [Knuth] less than or equal to three septated twice, $\leq g(6, 2, 3)$
smarithmonym: [sm- + arithmonym] word which becomes a number name if doubly beheaded: alone, atone, clone, crone, drone, ozone, phone, prone, scone, shone, ...
smeerp syndrome: [call a rabbit a smeerp] unthought-out creativity
smelic: [smell + lick portmanteau] referring to licking and smelling at the same time
Smith's Law: "No real problem has a solution; a solvable problem is not worth solving."
smoff: [secret master of fandom acronym] acting like a know-it-all
sneezure: [sneeze seisure portmanteau] fit of several sneezes in a row
snirt: [paleologism] laugh that turns into a snort
snod: [paleologism] (make) smooth, trim, neat, orderly
snool: [paleologism] cringe, cringer
snow-fall: [hyphenym] premature wintry weather
snowball: increasing in size letter by letter

snowbored: [snowboard mondegreen] unable to concentrate on anything but having or not having enough snowfall accumulation for a snowday
soblong: [sob + oblong portmanteau] describing a soft, drawn-out crying session
sociable: [P. Poulet] numbers whose factors add to next in chain
socitnropt: [Hazlitt acronym] "Simplicity of character is the natural result of profound thought."
socratease: [Socrates + tease portmanteau] Socrates-like leading question
Sodd's Law: "The task thwarter is also thwarted."
soganghika: [Sanskrit] ten-to-the-ninty-first, ninety-oneplex, 10^{91}
sol: ["Sol omnibus lucet." acronym] The sun shines upon us all.
solem: [curtailed solemn] peaceful, serene, but not quite so silent in the end
solid: [square : cube :: polygon : ?] words which can be represented as at the vertices of a polydron: for tetrahedron: eat, sat, sea, set
sonnet: *Cent Mille Milliards de poèmes* by Raymond Queneau (estimated million centuries to read) ten possibilities for each of 14 verses
sorting: transformation of number into one with digits increasing rightward, analogous to alphone for acronyms
sosie: [Fren.] twin or counterpart
spacecraft: [mondegreen] art of shaping space by the placement of matter
spalindrome: word that would be a palindrome if initial letter were deleted, aka fore-anchored palindrome
specificity: true-negative rate of a test, see sensitivity and background
spelling rhyme: rhyme made by spelling out word rather than pronouncing it: " "Mary had a c-a-t, c-a-t, c-a-t with fur r-e-d and every where that Mary'd go the cat would t-o-o."
Spencer's Law: "Every cause produces more than one effect."
Spenserian sonnet: 14 verses rhymed $(ab)^2(bc)^2(cd)^2e^2$
sphinx: [Grk. "strangler"] long, long poem recited in one breath as in musical comedy patter-song: "The Nightmare Song of the Lord High Chancellor" in Iolanthe by Gilbert and Sullivan
spiky: [pi in sky wordle] mathematical eucatastrophe
Spock's Law: [Benjamin Spock."] "You know more than you think you know."
spolynyms: words except for an extra initial letter like ones with two or more of the characteristics of aannym, allonym, ambinym, ananym, anatonym, antonym, apostronym, aptronym, arithmonym, boustrophenym, capitonym, consonym, contronym, domunym, exonym, euonym, feminyms, grammanym, heteronym, homonym, iatronym, liponym, malonym, meronym, morsonym, naanym, ouijanym, pianonym, retronym, roonym, synonym, tautonym, telephonym, toonym
sponsible: [Lat. spons-] having the ability to sponse or espouse
spoonergram: word or phrase that is another's spoonerism: nearby? = beer nigh?, optimistically = misty optically, running cat = cunning rat, see orthinolgy
spoonerism: [Rev. William Archibald Spooner] transposition of phonemes in two or more words: "blushing crow"; "camel passing through the knee of an idol", "Crock of ages, left for me"; "I've had tee many martoonis."; "kisstomary to cuss the bride": "queer old dean"; "shoving leopard"; "This pie is occupued; allow me to sew you another sheet."; "well-boiled icicle"; "When the boys come home from France, we'll have the hags flung out.", see forkism and knifism
spooniferism: [spoonerism + kniferism portmanteau] switching of both initial consonant and vowel clusters

sporkniferism: [sporkism + knifism portmanteau] switching of clustered final and initial consonants and vowel clusters

sprhyme: [spelling rhyme portmanteau] rhyme made by spelling out word rather than pronouncing it: "Mary had a c-a-t with fur r-e-d and everywhere that Mary'd go the cat would t-o-o."

spuddle: [paleologism] make a fuss over triviality

square: n[2] n-letter words arranged to read both horizontally and vertically: "Rotas opera tenet Arepo sator." which is also a palindrome and a word cross of "paternoster" with two As and two Os at the arms; (2x2) ma, am; in, no; (3x3) ear, rea, are; oft, foe, ten; tea, ate, eat; use, sue, eel (4x4) come, oval, mass, else; dear, else, asps, rest; hope, opal, palm, elms; lane, area, near, ears; post, oboe, soon, tent; reap, else, asia, pear; rend, erie, nice, deer; slam, lama, amen, many; tide, idea, dear, ears; twit, were, iron, tent; wisp, into, stop, pops; (5x5) beach, enure, auger, creed, herds; chant, homer, amuse, nests, trees; parts, about, route, tutor, stern; sated, atone, toast, ensue, deter; space, pagan, agent, canoe, enter; sport, pacer, ochre, rerun, trend; warts, await, radar, tiara, straw; waste, actor, stone, tonic, erect; (7x7) mergers, eternal, regatta, gravity, entitle, rattler, slayers; (9x9) fraternies, regimental, agitative, titanitites, emanatist, retitrate, initiartor, eavestone, slestered [Wayne M. Goodwin]

square poem: [Jean Lescure] exploits all possible permutations of four(or n2) words: 1234, 1243, 1324, 1342, 2134, 2143, 2314, 2341, 2431,2413, 3124, 3142, 3214, 3241, 3412, 3421, 4123, 4132, 4213, 4231, 4312,4321

square word: word with square wordnum product, ad, add, ass, I, pap, ...stair

string: words formed by alternate equally sized beheadings and tailings compressed into a string: "shrimpairwaylayman" = "shrimp, impair, airway, waylay, layman" or "spaleatea" = "spa, ale, lea, eat, ate, tea"

ssorg: [gross ananym] reverse gross, four hundred forty-one

sta: ["Subucula tua apparet." acronym ("Your slip is showing.] You're exposing a flaw.

stam: [Hebrew] just because that is the way it is, not quite the same as davka

stanyportorm: [any port in storm wordle] less than ideal refuge

Stapp's paradox: "The universal aptitude for ineptitude makes any human accomplishment an incredible miracle."

statant: [paleologism] standing in profile

statelily: [stately + -ly compound] in a stately manner

stately: describes word using state abbreviation letters (usbigrams or ustrigrams): alkylamide, candid, car, flaky, gal, hid, malarial, mar, marine, memorial, mid, mil, per, rid, war, win, see borderstate

statohumorous: [stratocumulus cloud + status + humorous portmanteau] describes clown both satirical and humorous

statoserious: [cirrostratus cloud + serious + status portmanteau] describes clown that is both serious and satirical and not so humorous

stereotyping: basing conclusion on too small a sample

Stigler's Law: No scientific discovery is named after its original discoverer.

stinky pinky: rhyming-pair: "best jest, "dramatic fanatic" 'flower power", "In a while, crocodile!", "Later, alligator!", "loose goose", "mell-mell", "willy-nilly"

stirp: [paleologism] lineage

stive: [stiver (1/20 gulder) back-formation] become worth less

stiwih: [Rabelais acronym] "strike the iron whilst it's hot."

stoppertunity: [stopper + opportunity portmanteau] what might have been but wasn't, see winshield

strike-out: word left when even letters alternade or barbarism are deleted: bat (beauty), bite (bristle), boat (buoyant), bra (bureau), brains (barbarianisms), clips (calliopes), fat (feast), pet (presto), tinily (triennially)

string: word chain compressed into non-word: bagemud = bag + age + gem + emu + mud, conearideach = cone + near + arid + ride + idea + each, spalegobink = spa + pal, ale + leg + ego + gob + bin+ ink; vastonerichump = vast,+ stone + toner + rich + chump

Strong's Law: "There are not enough small numbers to enable an observer to recognize pattern from coincidence."

Stroop effect: [J. R. Stoop] difficulty in distinguishing two numbers numerical size increases if one is physically larger

stumm: [paleologism] quiet

sub-bourbon: [suburban mondegreen] inferior whiskey, moonshine, rotgut

suber: [rebus anaym, pl. iber] rebus read backward: K = one K = keno, B = solo B = bolos

subitization: ability to take in four objects at once

subtransadded: retaining the same letter value product when transadded

subtransdeleted: retaining the same letter value priduct when transdeleted

subtranspositioned: retaining the same letter value product when transpositioned: 56 = and, hag; 300 = beef, cabby, cede, doe, ell, job, lay, lee, ode, to, ...; 5,940 = five, lock; 152,880 = madonna, Madalene; 379,050 = Jesus, Messiah; 1,759,590 = genius, madness; 4,928,040 = immoral, sinful

sugar cane: [mondegreen] sweet, edible walking stick

Suhor's Law: A little ambiguity never hurts, (not like none or much.)

suitonym: [suit + pseudonym portmanteau] word with the letters in playing card suits (a, b, c, d, e, h, i, l, m, n, o, p, r, s, t, u): almond, club, diamond, ear, earth, heart, spa, spade

sum word: smaller word formed from larger one by adding letter alphabet counts in pairs: can = 3 + 1 + 15 = 4 + 16 = do

sumnum: [sum word extrapolation] smaller number formed by adding digit pairs of larger number: 11 from 101

super-charade: word that can divide into many other small words: antidisestablismentarianism = ant + id + is + es + tab + li + sh + men + tari + an + ism

super-root: number which has been tetrated, $n = srt_{n'}(^n n)$

superseed: [supercede mondegreen] sow at high-velocity

superultramegalosequipedalian: describing a word greater than ultramegalosesquipedalian (29 letters)

superultramegaloziticorumbatous: [superultramegalosesquipedalian + zitcorumbatous portmanteau] describing 31-letter nonce word

suplacen: [place in sun wordle] pleasant location

sup-position: [supper + position portmanteau] placement around the supper table

surd: number expressible with finite number of multiplications, additions or root extractions

surfiction: [Raymond Federman] deliberately illogical, incoherent, irrational, non sequitur and unrealistic, like Franz Kafka or James Joyce

surprise: pleasant when assumed falsehood is unexpectedly proved true, unpleasant when assumed truth is unexpectedly proved false, see Unexpected Paradox

surregular: overly irregular conjugations: bathtubim (bathtub), beeth (booth), beleption (believe), bote (bite), chost (choose), cose (cat), dra (drum), flang (fling), foxen (fox), greption

(grieve), hice (house), loke (leak), lood (land), lynges (lynx), meese (moose), mid (moo), photographim (photograph), plew (play), praught (preach), smold (smell), son (sin), tew (tie)
susu: ["Semper ubi sub ubi." acronym] Always where under where. (Always wear underwear everywhere.)
svaa: ["Si vis amaria, ama."acronym] If you wish to be loved, love.
switchword: [Sam Loyd, 1899; Henry Ernest Dudeney] word which is partially palindromic and partially tautonymous: roughwrought, huggermugger, interpreting, sensuousness
swither: [paleologism] doubt, waver
syllepsis: using one word with two others, each with a different meaning
symbol sense: [Lynn Arthur Steen] ability to use symbols (as in algebra, geometry) both abstractly and practically
syncope: dropping of letters or syllables in word or expression
synonum: [synonym back-formation] different but equivalent number name or expression
synecdoche: using part for the whole
synonimble: combination synonyms and pun, genuine chopper = real ax =relax
synonym chain: BLACK, dark, obscure, hidden, concealed, snug, comfortable, easy, simple, pure, WHITE; FIRST, head, climax, top, extreme, LAST; UGLY, offensive, insulting, insolent, proud, lordly, stately, grand, gorgeous, BEAUTIFUL; WRITER, scribe, clerk, scholar, academic, lecturer, READER
syntagm: sentence fragment
synthetic rhyme: rhyme with identical orthography, "snow, gow" for "snow, go"
t-devoiced: describes words with t changed to d: tab (dab), taffy (daffy), tale (dale), tamp (damp)
T-graphable: [triangle, Leonard Gordon] graphable as if on triangular tiling: area
t-invariant: describes words with t only in the 20th place: anarchoindividualist
Tactus' Law: "The unknown always passes for the marvelous."
Tagari: describes words which change to another word when a double vowel with a t between is reduced to the vowel: biting (bing), cutup (cup), photonic (phonic), see Af Jinni
tail: final digit of a number, line of poem or letter of word, see curtailment
taisui: [Jap.] ten-to-the-seventy-seventh, seventy-secondplex, 10^{77}
taisuigasha: [kou : kougasha :: taisui : ?] ten-to-the-ninety-second, ninety-twoplex,10^{92}
take-away: operation that combines subtraction and/or deletion:
talespin: [tailspin mondegreen] slightly biased version of story
tall division: [antonym of short division] hypermathematical division of numeral: 11 by 2 yields 1
tallakshana: [Sanskrit] ten-to-the-fifty-third, fifty-threeplex, 10^{53}
tallying: operation which lists number of times a digit is used as in autobiographical or biographical numbers or DENEAT
tammiawaaw: [Aesop acronym] "There's as much malice in a wink as a word."
tan renga: [Jap.] poem or number with 5 + 7 + 5 + 2(7) = 31 syllables
tanka: [Jap.] poem or number with 2(5 + 7) + 7 = 31 syllables
tapallage: [patallage patallage] patallage with first and third letters exchanged
tariffic: [tariff + terrific portmanteau] with a great balance of trade
tartle: [Scottish] fail to remember something that you reasonably ought to, like the name of a familiar person or thing
tastapfe: [Aesop acronym] "There's a time and place for everything."
taswosaw: [Aesop acronym] "They also serve who only stand and wait."

taswoty: [Aesop acronym] "There's always someone worse off than yourself."

tatfat: [Shakespeare acronym] "There's a time for all things."

tautogrammic chain: assassin, barbaric, chihuahua, Cincinatian, instantaneous, jinglingly, kinking, Louisianian, Miamian, naysays, nonconcern, nonionized, nonsense, obsesses, paleogeography, ratcatcher, redeeded, satiation, so-so solution, stomachache, supersuperb, ta-ta take care

tautonum: [tautonym back-formation] number with two identical frags

tautonym: word with two identical frags: bouncy-bouncy, mama, papa, per-second-per-second, poohpooh, so-so, ta-ta, toot-toot

taxic: [toxic + tax portmanteau] intolerable burden of taxation

teau: [from "teauport", "teauportman"] frag used in making a portmanteau by a teauporting teauportman: smog's og, smoke's smo, brunch's unch

teauport: [teauportman back-formation] form a portmanteau by linking two words anagrammarly by moving a word fragment to the end of a word

teauportman: [portmanteau syllable anagram] one who teauports

teater: [teeter mondegreen]

technillogical: [illogical + technological] having to do with illogical technology like the manufacture of weapons of mass or environmental destruction

technobabble: technological double talk

teeny-weeny: between itsy-bitsy and teensy-weensy (10 letters)

teensy-weensy: slightly larger (12 letters) than teeny-weeny

telananyms: [Dave Morice's telephone reversal] words with reversed telephone number equivalents: films (34567) and solid (76543)

telecrastination: [telephone procrastination portmanteau] letting the phone ring at least twice before answering

telephonym: [Dmitri Borgmann's telephone word] word with only traditional telephone letters, that is, without q or z, see keypunch

telephonum: telephone number equivalent which a number name transforms into: one = 663, two = 896, three = 84,733

telesynonyms: [telephone synonym] words with same telephone number equivalents: 228 = act, bat, cat

teletautonym: word with repeating telephonum pattern: limpkins (54,675,467), murmurous (687,687,687), trusts (878,787)

telisogram: [telephone + isogram portmanteau] word with 6 or 8 letters without repeating telephone number equivalents: earthly (3278489), police (765423), sodality (76325489)

tellerprompter: [teller + teleprompter portmanteau] bank teller that tells those waiting at one window that another window is available

telletiquette: [teller + etiquette portmanteau] adherence to the socially acceptable distance from another using an automatic teller machine (so as not to be suspected of trying to glimpse that person's password)

telligence: [intelligence back-formation] inability to learn

temperment: final sum of digit-squares, which reduces natural numbers to either one (choleric), four (sanguine), seven (melancholic), or nine (phlegmatic)

tenineight: [eight + nine + ten portmanteau] eight/nine/ten

tenon: [nonet ananym] poem with $1 + 2 + 3 + 4 + 5 + 6 + 7 + 8 + 9 = 45$ syllables rhyming $a^3b^2c^2d^2$

teotwawki: [acronym] the end of the world as we know it

terbangro: [interrobang wordle] combination interrogatory and exclamation mark

tercet: rhymed aaa

Terman's Law: The correlation between the quality and cost of education is negligible.

terminal: either head or tail

terza rima: rhymed aba bcb cdc …

testimoany: [testimony + moany portmanteau] telling the truth but whining about having to do so

tetempestapot: [tempest in teapot wordle] big problem where there shouldn't be any

tetration: [Rucker] operation just higher than exponentiation, multiple exponentiation, stacking exponents

textorcism: [text + exorcism] attempt to banish a terrible or frightening book from one's thoughts

textyle: [text + style portmanteau ≈ textile] choice of font

th-debuccalized: describes words whose th phoneme changed to h: there (hair), that (hat), thatch (hatch), Thee (he), them (hem), they (hey), though (ho)

thabto: [John Heywood acronym] "Two heads are better than one."

thatdoth: [acronym] "The head's always the dupe of the heart."

thealogy: goddess theology

threeesque: [three + -esque] word with three identical consecutive letters or number with three identical consecutive digits

thehangre: [hang in there wordle] encouraging word to persevere

theorious: [theory + serious portmanteau] phenomenon with many theories

thoroughfair: [thoroughfare mondegreen] both fairly thorough and thoroughly fair at the same time

thought experiment: experimenting that is pure thinking

threnodials: words using only eleven most frequent letters (those in threnodials), one, but not two, four, five, six, seven, eight, eleven

thrun: [Joseph Bowden] 13 (base 10) in base 16, symbolized by reversed

thyme clock: [time clock mondegreen] clock for timing thyme

tiabmim: [Keats acronym] "There is a budding morrow in midnight."

tiat: [1 Cor 9:25 acronym] "Temperate in all things."

tiborh: [acronym] "There is but one race, humanity."

tiegram: two words tied together by a letter to form a new word: air(e)dale, art(i)choke, back(g)round, bear(s)kin, belie(v)able, bet(o)ken, bull(e)tin, cable(g)ram, can(n)on, car(o)using, cock(t)ail, convent(i)on, deer(s)kin, disc(l)aim, ea(r)shot, ever(y)body, eye(g)lass, fair(y)land, far(m)yard, fool(s)cap, forge(t)fully, gun(b)oat, gun(s)hot, hand(i)work, imp(o)sing, know(l)edge, man(s)ion, pen(i)tent, never(m)ore, now(a)days, over(c)oat, rain(c)oat, sap(p)hire, scare(c)row, she(a)the, sin(g)song, step(m)other, tea(r)drop, torn(a)do, tread(m)ill, war(e)house, yell(o)wish

tie-raid: [tirade mondegreen] run on a clothing store during necktie sale

tiem: [Mary Baker Eddy paraphrase acronym] "Truth's immortal; error mortal."

tilhapig: [Voltaire acronym] "The infinitely little have a pride infinitely great."

Tillis' principle: "If you file it, you'll know where it is but never need it; if you don't file it, you won't know where it is, but will need it."

timawp: [Thomas Brooks acronym] "Truth is mighty and will prevail."

time span: [186,282.4x5,280/10^{-9}] about a foot/nanosecond

timstitche: [stitch in time wordle] apropos correction

tinaacic: [Aesop acronym] "There is no arguing a coward into courage."
tinegobbtmis: [Shakespeare acronym] "There is neither good or bad, but thinking makes it so."
tinela: [Disraeli acronym] "There is no education like adversity."
tinguish: [extinguish back-formation] set on fire
tinggwamom: [Aristotle acronym] "There i no great genius without a mixture of madness."
tinstawl: [Beecher acronym] "There is no such thing as white lies."
tipnhob: [Emerson acronym] "There is properly no history, only biography."
tireur a la ligne: ["puller on the line"] interpolating successively 1, 2, 4, 8, ... new sentences into text, *Les Coups du tireur ... la ligne enapocalypse lent, occup, ... lire 'Monnaie de singe"* *de William Faulkner* by Jacque Duchateau
tirequill: small rubbery protrusions on new tires
Titan: [Samuel Yates] discoverer of titanic prime
titanic: [Samuel Yates] with at least ten thousand digits
titl: [Prv 3:5 acronym] "Trust in the Lord.", see jot
titlambha: [Sanskrit] ten-to-the-twenty-ninth, twenty-nineplex, 10^{29}
tli: [acronym] too little information
tliwohr: [acronym] "The laborer is worthy of his reward."
tmesis: insertion of one or more words between parts of a compound word: abso-blooming-lutely, any-old-where, a-whole-nother, hoo-bloody-ray, some-other-where
toffer: [toffee back-formation] that which stretches toffee either Human or mechanical
toflag: [David Everett acronym] "Tall oaks from little acorns grow."
togethereness: [togetherness + there portmanteau] purpose of a family trip
Tom Swiftie: [Tom Swift series by Edward Stratemeyer] punning use of quote's adverb, "'Aren't five cups from one teabag a bit much,' Tom asked weakly.", "'Care to ride in my new ambulance?' Tom invited hospitably.","'Does this invisibility formula work?' Tom asked transparently.", 'I'm one happy camper,' Tom said intently.", "'I've lost my boutonniere' Tom said lackadaisically.", "'I've eaten William.' said the cannibal willfully.", "'Thank God my transplant took!' Tom said wholeheartedly.","'There's too much vermouth in this martini,' Tom said dryly."
toolsh: [toolshed back-formation] fill to overflowing
toonym: two-tailed homonym with silent last letter: too, add, bee, belle, block, borne, butt, bye, canvass, caste, damn, flue, fore, inn, lamb, lapse, ore, please, sow, wee
topnotch: highest adult height, full-growth
toregami: [tore + orogami portmanteau] art of paper-folding that allows tearing the paper
Torquemada's Law: [Tomás de Torquemada] "When you are right, you have a moral duty to impose your will on everyone who is wrong."
tonguetide: [tongue-tied mondegreen] off-and-on verbosity
tonguetwister: [*Peter Piper's Practical Principles of Plain and Perfect Pronunciation* 1834] "How many cans can a cannibal nibble, if a cannibal can nibble cans?", "How many tall tales'll the tall tall tale teller tell, when the tall tall tale teller tells tall tales?", "If Peter Piper picked a peck of pickled peppers, how many pecks of pickled peppers did Peter Piper pick?", "If Neddie Noodle nipped his neighbor's nutmegs, where are the nutmegs Neddy Noodle nipped?", "If Oliver Oglethorp ogles an owl and an oyster, where are the owl and oyster Oliver Oglethorp ogled?", "If she sells seashells by the seashore, how many seashells by the seashore did she sell?", "How much wood would a woodchuck chuck, if a woodchuck could chuck wood?", (Carolyn Wells' limericks) "A canner exceedingly canny One morning

remarked to his granny, 'A canner can can Anything that he can, But a canner can't can a can, can he?'", "A tutor who tooted the flute Tried to tutor two tutors to toot. Said the two to the tutor, 'Is it harder to toot, or To tutor two tutors to toot?'"

tonic: describes a weight close (±10%) to a ton or metric tonne

too-sense: [two cents mondegreen] dis/confirmation of a sensible idea

Tood and Janey Effect: [Doc Webster, quoted by Spider Robinson, on presumably illiterate concrete poet named Todd] dumbing down

topheavy: ["Countdown"] with a title greater than text: "The Marine Clairvoyant's Reply to a Query Concerning Her Occupation" I Eye."

toroviv: [Emerson acronym] "The only reward of virtue is virtue.", see hitrov

tow-headed: [towheaded hyphenym] describing a word beginning with tow- but not referring to tow: toward, towel, towelette, tower, town, townsfolk

towtbafitbo: [Emerson acronym] "The only way to be a friend is to be one."

TQ: [telligence quotient, IQ back-formation] measure of inability to learn

transaddition: [transposition addition portmanteau] inverse operation to transdeletion by which a word or number is related to its "ancestral" word or number

transcendental: [Joseph Liouville] describing a number not the root of any polynomial with rational coefficients

transcode: encoding and decoding between different expressions, such as spoken, heard, seen, written numbers or decimals, fractions, quotients

transdeletion: [transposition deletion portmanteau] operation turning a word or number into a "descendant" word or number by deletion(s) and/or transposition(s) of letter(s) or digit(s), as in TEN from FOURTEEN or 10 from 101

transfinite: [Gregor Catnor] number higher than finite, the first of which is aleph-null

transpositioned: symbolized by changed order in parentheses: lien (1243) line, line (1243) lien, ate (231) tea (231) eat (231) ate, cimematographer (54961D2X8E74X63) megachiropteran

transprose: prose from verse

transumptive: metaphorically substituted term

transverse: verse from prose

traulism: travesty: [transvestism contraction] kind of burlesque with either nonsense dignified and formal or the serious trivialized: *Perfect Behavior* by Donald Ogden Stewart

traynee: [tray + trainee portmanteau] newbee waiter/waitress

trazillion: [trillion + -az-] indeterminate number higher than a bazillion of the form ten-z-ated-to-the-twelfth, g(z, 12, 10)

treaty: [back-formation] having to do with treats like snacks or deserts

tree: diagram connecting a words root transdeletions and branch transadditions: olympic's impolicy, myopical, olympics, polemic and myopical and comply, imploy, myopic, policy

Treppenwitz: [German] witty remark, perfect reparté remembered after opportune moment has passed

tresspass: [tress + trespass portmanteau] inappropriately touch someone else's hair

tri-dirt: [mynynym] mixture of three types of soil

tri-inary: refering to a number system based on 3i

triad: combination of three two-word phrases into a three-word phrase: last minute waltz, silver sand dollar, white light house, see tricycle

trial lawyer: [mondegreen] attorney on probation

trialphabetical: describes word able to be separated into just three alphabetical sequences: word = w + or + d or alphabet = alpt + h + abe

tricephalous: describes word beheadable two times before becoming a nonword: core, cram, grace, heat, here, islander, lion, oman, owing, pore, scat, scowl, selector, stern, stray, trash, trend, upraise, [Ogden Nash, lamma : llama :: llama : ?] lllama, lllano, lllave, lllover

tricicle: [triple + icicle portmanteau] icicle with three points

tricycle: three words which can form three two-word phrases and/or compound(s): saw horse power

trimming: reducing all digits by one and dropping zeros, changes googol to zero (!)

trinade: [2 : 3 :: binade : ?] word able to be broken by taking letters in threes into 3 words: pacificatory = pico + afar + city

Trinary Law: There are three kinds of people in the world, those who can count and those who can't.

trintts: [Eccl 9:11 acronym] "The race is not to the swift."

triolet: [Fren.] rhymed aba^{3}bab, where a is same identical rhyming word

trioomph: [triumph + oomph portmanteau] victory that require extra effort

triplet: [doublet extrapolation] changing one word to another two letters at a time

triplogram: word with every letter repeated twice: deeded, geggee, sestettes

triskaidekaphobia: abnormal fear of thirteen

triskaidekaphobiacophobia: abnormal fear of being triskaidekaphobiac

trisograms: three words with no letters in common: dumping, freshly, jackbox

trit: [two : bit :: three : ?] base three information unit

trivial: taught in the prerequisite class

tro: [million : mo :: trillion : ?] third great gross, twelve-to-the-fifth, 12^5 = 248,832, rare large last-half number name which uses just letters alphabetically after M

tropical illusion: [tropical + optical illusion portmanteau] daydream about a vacation one is likely never going to go on

trouble-shooting: [troubleshooting mondegreen] trying to fire a malfunctioning firearm

Truly Large Number Law: With a large enough sample many odd coincidences become likely.

truncatable: able to retain property even after beheadable and curtailable

truthbrush: [truth + toothbrush portmanteau] self-deceiver's close encounter with Truth

tsarr: [Goethe acronym] "Thou shalt abstain, renounce, refrain."

tsiapais: [Pascal acronym] "The stream is always purer at the source."

tsigologist: [-ologist mynynym] student of palindromes and/or numberdromes

tsoasip: [Xenophon acronym] "The sweetest of all sounds is praise."

ttsas: [Aesop acronym] "To the selfish all're selfish."

tu quoque: fallacy of returning ad hominem for ad hominem

tug of peace: [tug of war antonym] relentless urge of a dove (peacemaker) not shared by a hawk (warmonger)

tug of war: [mondegreen] relentless urge of a hawk (warmonger) not shared by a dove (peacemaker)

tulp: ["Transit umbra, lux permanet." acronym] The shadow passes, the light remains (on the sun dial.)

turnament: [tournament mondegreen] vehicle steering competition

Turner's Law: Nearly 100% of public prophesies are wrong.

twee: [tweed back-formation]

twelveleven: [eleven + twelve portmanteau] eleven/twelve
twelfty: [J. Michael Straczynski] ten dozens, 120
twialumf: [Ps 118:105 acrnym] "Thy word is a lamp unto my feet."
twin end: word with same letter(s) on ends: (1) absentia, acacia, academia, ... (2) alembical, alimental, allowal, church, deride, desuetude, edified, edited, educated, enliven, escapades, escapes, esquires, estates, headache, insulin, leavable, orator, photograph, sense, shellfish, teammate, temperate, terminate, verve; (3) entanglement, entertainment, enticement, entrancement, ingeminating, ingesting, ingraining, ingratiating, ingrossing, ingurgitating, ingrowing, ionization, restores, (4) hoodlumhood, lessonless, shipownership
twistare: [twist + stare portmanteau ≈ twister] staring at a twist-tie while twisting back and forth until one finds the correct direction to untwist it
twosid: [Rom 7:23 acronym] "The wages of sin is death."
twotih: [Prv 13:15 acronym] "The way of transgressors is hard."
twotoo: [tutu homonym] also a couple
twone: [two + one portmanteau] one/two
twychild: [twy + child compound] old person in second childhood
twystery: [twist + mystery portmanteau] mystery story with a surprise ending
Tylk's Law: Assumption is the mother of foul-ups.
U: [Hon. Nancy Mitford] upperclass English dialect: Barkshire, black tie, cinema, clark, counterpane, Darby, dinner jacket, frightfully, go'f, how d'you do?, jam, kinsman, lavatory paper, looking-glass, master, mistress, nice, sorry, tails, vegetables, white tie, woman, writing paper
U-keili: describes word with only u as vowel: church, cumulus, cupful, fulcrum, fungus, guru, humbug, skunk, spud, suburb, sulfur, surplus, tutu, unjust, untrustful, untruthful
ubious: ["(Yo)u b(elieve) i(t!)" grammanym back-formation] disbelieving that another believes
ubebious: ["(Yo)u b(elieve) e(veryone) b(elieves) i(t)!" grammanym back-formation] disbelieving that another believes that all others believe
ubibious: ["(Yo)u b(elieve) I b(elieve) i(t!)" grammanym back-formation] disbelieving that another believes that you believe
ubidbious: ["(Yo)u b(elieve) I d(on't) b(elieve) i(t!)" grammanym back-formation] disbelieving that another believes that you disbelieve
ubidious: ["(Yo)u b(elieve) I d(isbelieve) i(t!)" grammanym back-formation] disbelieving that another believes that you disbelieve
ubious: ["(Yo)u b(elieve) i(t!)" grammanym back-formation] disbelieving that another believes
ububious: ["(Yo)u b(elieve) yo)u b(elieve) i(!)" grammanym back-formation] disbelieving that another believes that they believe
ubudbious: ["(Yo)u b(elieve yo)u d(on't) b(elieve) i(!)" grammanym back-formation] disbelieving that another believes that they disbelieve
ubudious: ["(Yo)u b(elieve yo)u d(isbelieve) i(!)" grammanym back-formation] disbelieving that another believes that they disbelieve
udabious: ["(Yo)u d(isbelieve) a(nyone) b(elieves) i(t!)" grammanym back-formation] disbelieving that other disbelieves that any disbelieve
Udall's Law: "If everyone agrees, it's wrong.", see Valéry's Law
udbabious: ["(Yo)u d(isbelieve) a(nyone) b(elieves) i(t!)" grammanym back-formation] not believing that another disbelieves that any others believe
udbebious: ["(Yo)u d(on't) b(elieve) e(veryone) b(elieves) i(t!)" grammanym] not believing that another does not believe that all others do believe

udbibious: ["(Yo)u d(on't) b(elieve) I b(elieve) i(t.)" grammanym back-formation] not believing that another does not believe that you do believe
udbubious: ["(Yo)u d(on't) b(elieve yo)u b(elieve) i(t!)" grammanym back-formation] not believing another does not believe that they believe
udderly: [udder back-formation ≈ utterly] hanging or dangling in a squishy manner
udebious: ["(Yo)u d(on't) b(elieve) e(veryone) b(elieves) i(t!)" grammanym back-formation] not believing that another does not believe that all others do believe
udibious: ["(Yo)u d(on't) b(elieve) I b(elieve) i(t.)" grammanym back-formation] not believing that another does not believe that you do believe
udnananeermh: [Voltaire acronym] "Use, do not abuse; neither abstinence not exces ever renders man happy."
udubious: ["(Yo)u d(on't) b(elieve yo)u b(elieve) i(t!)" grammanym back-formation] not believing another does not believe that they believe
uf: [uberrimae fidei] of utmost good faith
uheible: ["Ubicumque homo est, ibi benefici locus est." acronym] Wherever there is a man, there is a place of/for kindness/service
uheiblity: ability to be kind or serve
ufii: [Ubi fumus ibi ignis. acronym] Where there's smoke there's fire.
ulceration: [George Perec] using only the 11 most frequent letters in French
Ulmann's Razor: "When stupidity is sufficient explanation, look no further.", see Hanlon's Razor
Ultimate Law: "One hundred percent of general statements are false, including this one."
ultramegalosesquipedal: describing a word longer than megalosesquipedalian (24 letters),
ultramegaloziticorumbatous: [ultramegalosesquipedalian + zitcorumbatous portmanteau] describes 26-letter nonce word
umeo: [Usus magister est optimus. acronym] Practice makes perfect.
umia [Ubi mel ibi apes. acronym] Where there's honey, there's bees (and/or apes); if you want support, you must offer something in return.
UMO: [unaccountably moving objects acronym] things that move unexpectedly, like moving statues, walking trees, productive bureaucrats
umpteen: [telegraphers' jargon, ump + -teen] indeterminate number a little higher than a thousand, ≈ 1,010
umpty: [-teen : -ty :: umpteen : ?] indeterminate number about as high as a myriad, fourplex
unattractive: describes heteronymous antonyms: Adam (Eve), against (for), boy (girl), day (night), evil (good), father (son), husband (wife), lie (truth)
uncleonym: [auntonym antonym] name of one's parent's brother
unconditional: [mondegreen] without a medical condition, healthy
undicina: [*Ulérations* by Georges Perec] 121-versed quenina
underrounding: rounding to the right of significant digit
Unexpected Paradox: [W. V. Quine] possibility other than expected is always unexpected
unidigital: single-digited, between 0 and 9
uni-corn: [unicorn hyphenym] solitary thickening of the skin on a foot
univocal: with only one of the vowels: *The Fall of Eve*: "Eve, Eden's empress, needs defended be. The serpent greets her when she seeks the tree. Serene she sees the speckled tempter creep. Gentle he seems: perverted schemer deep: Yet endless pretexts, ever fresh, prefers. Perverts her senses, revels when she errs, Sneers when she weeps, regrets, repents, when she fell, deep revenged, re-seeks the netherhell.", "Persevere, ye perfect men,

ever keep the precepts ten."

univocalic: with only one of six vowels in the number name, as in two, three, six, seven, ten, eleven, twelve, seventeen, googol

unplode: [ex/implode back-formation] disarm a bomb without exploding or imploding

unpunctuated: text that can be read in different ways [Jesuitically] if punctuated: "Every lady in the land has twenty nails(;) on each hand five and twenty on hands and feet(;) this is true without deceit(.)", "I saw a peacock(;) with a fiery tail I saw a blazing comet (;) drop down hail I saw a cloud(;) burn up in fire I saw a house(;) big as the moon and higher I saw the sun(;) even in the midst of night I saw the man that saw this wondrous sight(.)"; "Women are pretty(,) generally speaking(.)"; "Thou shalt go(;) thou shalt return never(;) by war shalt thou perish(.)", "She, where he had had (")...(",) (")...(") had had too.", "She wrote that that (")...("), that (")...(") that he wrote, he wrote right(.)" [2n(6) + 4n = 6, 16, 36, 76, 156, 316, ...] "That that is is(;)not that that is not is not(;) that that is is not that that is not(;)that that is not is not that that is(;) that is it(,) is it not(?)"

unrest: [mondegren] every activity done while awake

untill: [until mondegreen] remove all the cash out of the cash register

upno: ["Ultra posse nemo obligatur." acronym] Beyond one's ability nobody's bound., see inoe

unce: [nonce back-formation] describes word without usual prefix: couth (uncouth), nocent (innocent)

undercover: [mondegreen] shelter it begins to rain or storm

undew: [undo mondegreen] what the warm sunlight does during the day that the cool air did during the night

undivided attention: attention given to a problem in long, side or tall division before the solution is found

unevenum: number with only odd digits

uneventide: odd hours of the day

unevenymous: [evenym ananym] describing word(s) with only the odd letters of the alphabet (a, c, e, g, i, k, m, o, q, s, u, w, y): Amy says Guy may seek easy wages as a quick cook.

Unian: [beheaded Dunian] with first first and last four lines unwritten

unicycle: two-syllable word able to swap syllables to become another word: German ≠ manger

univocalic: word with just one vowel: archcharlatans, defenselessness, letter, primitivistic, sentence, untruthful, word, syzygy

unlooped: with head turned into new tail

Unnamed Law: It happened, so it was not impossible.

unonymous: [unanimous + anonymous portmanteau] with all secret ballots in agreement

unooled: [ool antonym] re-headed and then looped

unooped: [oop antonym] re-headed and then pooled

unpooled: [pooled antonym] reversed and then looped

unrational: number able to transform rational number to irrational or vice versa

unreal: ambiguous number like to-the-second-i, $^i i$

"unrhymable": breadth [dreadth], month [(n+1)th], orange [corn j-(uice)]; chimney [Jim's knee], circle [jerk'll], desert [Dee's hurt], monarch [nonnark], virtue [her too], wisdom [msdom], "This intellectual Has doublechecked you all.", "I've just now bought two p- Ennyworth of soup.", "28 days to the month Does February runn'th.", "The prophet Samuel rode on his camuel."

Unspeakable Law: As soon as you mention something, if it's good, it goes away. if it's bad, it happens.

up-arrow: ↑, symbol for exponentiation, when doubled, tetration, confusingly abbreviated in ASCI to caret, ^

upend: turn a story conclusion toward eucatastrophe, happy ending

uppala: [Sanskrit] ten-to-the-ninety-eighth, ninety-eightplex, 10^{98}

UQ: [unanswerable question] question stated so as to be impossible to answer, such as "What question is more difficult to answer than this one?"

urtailment: [Dmitri Borgmann's terminal deletion/beheaded curtailment] removal of both ends of a word: heart = ear, magenta = agent, revolver = evolve

urunimi: ["you are you and I am I" pseudo-acronym] principle of undependance which appreciated *la difference* between people, especially between I AM (God) and everyone else

usbigram: two-letter abbreviations of states (AK, AL, AR, AZ, CA, CO, CT, DE, FL, GA, HI, IA, ID, IL, IN, KS, KY, LA, MA, MD, ME, MI, MN, MO, MS, MT, NC, ND, NE, NH, NJ, NM, NV, NY, OH, OK, OR, PA, RI, SC, SD, TN, UT, VA, VT, WA, WI, WV, WY), see stately, border

ustrigram: two over-lapping usbigrams (AKS, AKY, ALA, ARI, CAK, CAL, CAR, CAZ, COH, COK, COR, CTN, FLA, GAK, GAL, GAR, GAZ, HIA, HID, HIL, HIN, IAK, IAL, IAR, IAZ, IDE, ILA, INC, IND, INE, INJ, INM, INV, INY, KSC, KSD, LAK, LAL, LAR, LAZ, MAK, MAL, MAR, MAZ, MDE, MIA, MID, MIL, MIN, MNC, MND, MNE, MNH, MNJ, MOH, MOK, MSC, MSD, MTN, NCA, NCO, NCT, NDE, NHI, NMA, NMD, NMI, NMN, NMO, NMS, NMT, NVA, NVT, OHI, OKS, OKY, ORI, PAK, PAL, PAR, PAZ, RIA, RID, RIL, RIN, SCA, SCO, SCT, SDE, TNC, TND, TNE, TNH, TNJ, TNM, TNV, TNY, UTN, VAK, VAL, VAR, VAZ, VTN, WAK, WAL, WAR, WAZ, WIA, WID, WIL, WIN, WVA, WVT), see stately

usece: ["Ubi Spiritus est cantus est." acronym] Where there's the Spirit there's song

usfim: ["Ut sementem feceris, ita metes." acronym] As you sow, so shall you reap; what goes around, comes around.

utpatap: [Tit 1:15 acronym] "Unto the pure all things are pure."

uttermost: [mondegreen] talk more than anyone else

uvruwuxuvru: [ABCD : UVWX :: abracadabra : ?] nonsense word like abracadabra

Vagari: describes words which change to another word when a double vowel with an I between is reduced to the vowel: diving (ding), event (ent), livid (lid), provost (post), see Af Jinni

Valéry's Law: "If it has always been accepted, it is almost certainly false.", see Udall's Law

vamel: [D'ni] twenty-five-to-the-ninth, not-so-little eighteenplex, $25^9 = 5^{18} = 3,814,697,265,625$

vampire: number with same digits as its factors ignoring terminating zeroes

van guard: [vangard mondegreen] security personnel hired to protect large vehicle

vappanci: [verb, adverb, pronoun, preposition, adjective, noun, conjunction, interjection acronymous mnemonic, sing. vappancus] parts of speech

vara: [D'ni] twenty-five-to-the-sixth, not-so-little twelveplex, $25^6 = 5^{12} = 244,140,625$

variation: usually taken as $\pm\sqrt{n}$

vas: [D'ni] twenty-five-to-the-seventh, not-so-little fourteenplex, $25^7 = 5^{14} = 6,103,515,625$

veinglorious: [vein + vainglorious portmanteau] describes when a prospector strikes the motherload

venerable: describes word beginning with ven- that generates a fictitious name, Ven. Etian, Ven. Ezuelan, Ven. Turous

venommess: [venomous + mess portmanteau] what happen when venom collector messes up

ventina: [George Perce] poem with 20^2 = 400 lines spirally rhymed
ventriloquest: [ventriloquist + quest portmanteau] search for laryngitis cure
Verdunian: truncated poem with with all but first line unwritten, but implied, as in limerick: "There once was a man of Verdun (Whose limericks ended at line one. He'd only begun To rhyme something with -un, When his limericking was done.)
vibhutangama: [Sanskrit] ten-to-the-fifty-first, fifty-oneplex,10^{51}
vicinal: [Eugene Ulrich] word of alphabetical neighbors: antidisestablishmentarianism, baa, becalmed, bedfast, bedlam, bighead, cab, cede, chide, chipboards, cohabitations, combatants, condemned, deeded, documents, done, fights , foments, hedonist, high-minded, hoiden, meddled, mooned, pompon, requested, rusts, sighted, sponsors, sports, stressed, struts, support, tabu, this, truss, trusts, tutus, undermost, unsought
vidience: [audio : video :: audience : ?] those who watch television, watchership
vihvis: [Petrach acronym] "Virtue is health; vice is sickness."
vijaya: [Indian] thirty million, 30,000,000
villanelle: [Fren.] poem with 5(3) + 4 = 19 verses
virtually impossible: not possible in VR, where anything conceivable is possible, inconceivable in thought experience
vivaha: [Sanskrit] ten-to-the-nineteenth, nineteenplex,10^{19}
vivara: [Sanskrit] ten-to-the-fifteenth, fifteenplex,10^{15}
volume: product of number's height, length and width
Vorval's number: [Lavrov ananym] reverse of Lavrov's number: one
vov: ["Vincit omnia veritas." acronym] Truth conquers all.
vowelindrome: [vowel + palindrome portmanteau] one of five palindromes with the same consonants but five different vowels: pap, pep, pip, pop, pup
vrinda: [Sanskrit] ten-to-the-twenty-seventh, twenty-sevenplex,10^{27}
vulture Up-to: ["What you up to?" 1970 *Time* contest] pun combining familiar phrase or saying with animal name as if a given or surname, Aardvard And-no-play-makes-Jack-a-dull-boy, Ape Ollo, Ape Ostrophy, Ape Ricot, Ape Rilfool, Ape Ron, Asia Myna, Bird Brain, Bird Ensome, Canary Islands, Cat Aclysm, Cat A-comb. Cat A-log, Cat Aleptic, Cat Alyst, Cat Apult, Cat Aract, Cat A-tonic, Cat Egory, Cat 'Er-pillar, Cat 'Er-wall, Cat Lick, Chick Ken, Chimp Pansy, Coca Koala, Cow Abunga, Cow Ard, Cuff Lynx, Dog Daze, Dog Earl, Dog Matic, Dolly Llama, Fish Sherman, Gorilla My-dreams, Hadn't Otter, Hippo Crit, Hippo Drome, Hippo Pot-a-moose, Monkey Business, Monkey Shines, Monkey Wrench, Mouse Kateer, One-good Tern, Ostrich In-time-saves-nine, Panda Monium, Piranha Old-grey-bonnet, Rat Chet, Rat Lars, Sea anemone Make-a-friend, Tabby Or-not-tabby, Toucan Live-as-cheaply-as-one, see knock-knock, perverb
vurge: [verbal + urge portmanteau] desire to write or speak
vyavasthanapjnapati: [Sanskrit] ten-to-the-thirty-first, thirty-oneplex,10^{31}
W ± n method: substituting a word a certain number before or after for the given word in a sentence, generalization of N + 7 method
wabi: [Japanese] distinctive flawed detail that creates an elegant, more beautiful, even uniquely beautiful, whole
wabswiooc: [Aesop acronym] "We are but sorry witnesses in our own cause."
Wagari: describes words which change to another word when a double vowel with an I between is reduced to the vowel: awash (ash), hewer (her), mewed (med), rewed (red), see Af Jinni

Walinsky's Law: Intelligence in a discussion is inversely proportional to the square of the number of people involved. (see Shanahan's Law)

wallflow: [wallflower back-formation] move back and forth along a wall without moving away from it

Walton's Second Law: No one can lose what he never had.

wamoltloh: [acronym] "When a man owns land the land owns him."

wamstshar: [acronym] "Whatever a man sow that shall he also reap."

want knot: [want not mondegreen] knot that is wanted, not wasted

war-headed: [warhead hyphenym] describing a word beginning with war- but not referring to war: warble, warbler, ward, warden, wardrobe, wardroom, warehouse, warlock, warm, warn, warp, warrant, warren, wart, warthog

waste knot: [waste not mondegreen] knot that is wasted, not wanted

watersh: [watershed back-formation] overflow, flood

watmom: [Carlyle acronym] "We are the miracle of miracles."

wavee: [wave back-formation ≈ wavy] person waver waves at

wayfairer: [wayfarer + fairer portmanteau] describes fellow traveler who is much more accommodating than you

weath: [weather back-formation] what weather does, change

weathervain: [weathervane + vain portmanteau] describes someone who thinks they know more about meteorology than they actually do

webby: [Edward MacNeal] knowledge collected to other knowledge into a knowledge web

wicked: [wicked mondegreen] describes candle or lantern with a wick

wei-wu-wei: [Chinese] conscious inaction, doing nothing at the proper time and for the proper reason

weight: sum of number's digits as in casting-out-nines (Hamming weight: sum in binary)

Weiler's Law: Nothing is impossible for the man who does not have to do it himself.

well-headed: [wellhead hyphenym, beheaded swellheaded] describing a word beginning with well- not referring to well: wellerism

wellerism: [Samuel Weller, *Pickwick Papers* by Charles Dickens, though in Samuel Beazley. 1811] enlivening of a cliché with creativity: "'We all have our little foibles', as the Frenchman said when he boiled his grandmother's head", "'Out with it', as the father said to the child when it swallowed a farthing."

wellf: [wellfed back-formation] fatten for slaughter

welterweight: refers to number with a weight between lightweight (zero) and middleweight (four and a half), $0 \le w_n \le 4.5$

Wendhamian: [from J. A. Lindon's Wendham poet's limerick] with final rhyme unwritten, but implied

Weskimen's Law: There is never enough time to do a thing right, but always enough time to do it over.

Westheimer's Law: Months in the laboratory is worth hours in the library. (720:1).

wetwawlia: [Froude acronym] "We enter the worl alone; we leave it alone."

wff: ["well-formed formula" three-letter acronym (tla), pronounced as, but not to be confused with, wiff] logical formula formed in accord with symbols, such as in Łukasiewicz-Bocheński "Polish" notation: Apq (p or q), Bpq (not p if q), Cpq (if p then q), Dpq (not p and q), Epq (p iff q), Jpq (p or q but not p and q), Kpq (p and q), Mp (maybe p), Np (not p), Op (p false), Vpq (p is q), Xpq (not p or q)

whent: [when + went portmanteau] chronoported

wherewithall: [wherewithal mondegreen] describes something position, what is with in and everything else about it

Whitehead's Law: "The obvious is often overlooked."

whoplot: [hoopla + plot portmanteau] pre-publication promotion of a who-dunit

wibig: [acronym] "What is beautiful is good."

wibit: [acronym] "What is beautiful is true."

widower: [widow back-formation] between widow and widowest

width: number name syllable count, approximation for duration of spoken number name for calculating number volume

wiff: [what-if contraction] alternative created by changing something

wigib: [acronym] "What is good is beautiful."

wigit: [acronym] "What is good is true."

wihii: [Bulwer-Lytton acronym] "What is Human is immortal!"

Wiltshire's Law: "To define is to limit."

Winogradow's number: to-the-fourth-e-to-the-forty-one-point-ninety-sixth, $^4e^{41.96}$

winshield: [win + windshield portmanteau] self-sabotaging mental block

winsome: usually charismatic unless losing

wird: [misspelled word, since i is closed vowel on keyboard to o] misspelled word

Wirth's law: "Software gets slower faster than hardware gets faster."

wis: [paleologism] know

Wisdom Law: Wisdom is considered a sign of weakness by the powerful because a wise man can lead without power, but only a powerful man can lead without wisdom.

witib: [acronym] "What is true is beautiful."

witig: [acronym] "What is true is good."

witimaamit: [Plautus acronym] "What is thine is mine and all mine is thine."

Wittgenstein's Law: "Of that of which nothing is known nothing can be said, except that 'That of which nothing is known nothing can be said.' cannot be said."

Wodagroniw's number: [Winogradow ananym] reverse of Winogradow's number, R($^4e^{41.96}$)

wotiagobcweo: [Ralph Waldo Emerson acronym] "Works of the intellect are great only by comparison with each other."

woofs: [well-off older folks acronym] wealthier elderly

Wolf's Law: The time and energy to undo a wrong is much greater than that to do one. (see Drazen's Law)

word chain: aka Chinese verse, series of words sharing the last letter(s) of the first with the first letter(s) of the next: bag, age, gem, emu, mud; cone, near, arid, idea, each; "At the ends several low words share."

word square: [word : words :: word square : ?] n-square words arranged in square: if magic: to form sentence(s):

my	dog	is	weak
dog	the	fighting	man
is	fighting	good	will
weak	man	will	fall

wordling: transformation of word into letter sequence rebus by transdeletion in which frags are taken literally: inches = in c, h es = cesh

wordling, nested: wordling with multiple transformations: atgastrostl (gastrointestinal), ecdisld (disinclined), eepephrs (epinephrines), egard (ingrained), eocrls (crinolines), etmaad (maintained), etstes (intestines), gdrekls (reinklings), gdwowdresss (windowdressings), gnwgds (wingdings), gksprls (sprinklings), gktwls (twinklings), nppots (pinpoints), oeantutrs (antineutrinos), tfskls (skinflints), tgerf-pags (finger-paintings), tgferprs (fingerprints)

wordnum: [Lee Sallow] value of word according to sum of letters' alphabetical positions, evaluated in base 27 (or 37), see balanced words

wordnym: word evaluated as wordnum in base 27 (or 37)

worfle: [Norm Storer] positive penumbral connotation, as in the successful yoof

worm: [Keith Jones, Grant Willson] vector sequence corresponding to the 26 directions of two half-cubes or "cubets" with abc, def, ghi on top; jkl, n, qpo, m around the middle and rst, uvw, xyz on the bottom, symbolized by the angle in degrees between parentheses and the squared distance(s): at = it = 3 (60) 3, go = if = 3 (150) 2, and = 3 (60) (45) 2

wowf: [paleologism] wild, crazed (wolf)

wrapture: [wrap + rapture portmanteau] ecstacy when one has all of one's Christmas presents wrapped

wrrd: word without vowels: brrr, Btfsplk, crwth, crwths, cwm, cwmtwrch, d--m, G-d, grr, grrl, h--l, hmm, Krk [Serbia], Llwchwr [Wales], nth, psst, pthwndxrclzp, tsk, tsktsk, xth, zth, zzz

wud: [Bugs Bunny acronym] What's up, doc?

wunty: [Joseph Bowden] 16 (base 10) in base 16

wurp: [paleologism] snubbable social inadequate

WYDSIWYG: ["What you don't see is what you get" acronym] principle that faith concerns things unseen so you get more than what you can see

WYSIWYG: ["What you see is what you get." acronym] principle of fairness that you get exactly what you see and not more

Wyszowski's Laws: (1) No experiment is reproducible. (2) Anything can be made to work if you fiddle with it long enough (but not if you do so too long)".

wytitwyhba: [acronym] "Where your treasure is there will your heart be also."

Xagari: describes words which change to another word when a double vowel with an x between is reduced to the vowel: apexes (apes), ex-egg, flexed (fled), see Af Jinni

xonym: [Dave Morice's tic-tac-toe word] 3-or-less-letter word with only x or o, as used in tic-tac-toe: o, oo, ooo, ox, oxo, oxx, x, xo, xoo, xox, xx, xxx

xor: [exclusionary or] logical operator or-but-not-and/or, disjunction but not conjunction

xyz: ["Examine your zipper." grammanym] your zipper is unzipped

xzwamfeujho: unpronounceable name for undefinable literary form

Y-keili: describes words with only y as a vowel: by, cry, crypt, cyst, dry, dryly, fly, flyby, fry, glycyl, glyph, gym, gypsy, hymn, lymph, lynch, lynx, my, myrrh, myth, nymph, ply, pry, psych, pygmy, pyx, rhythm, sylph, sync, synch, syzygy, try, tryst, why, wry, wryly, xylyl, xyst

yabmas: [acronym] "Youth's a blunder; manhood a struggle."

Yagari: describes words which change to another word when a double vowel with a y between is reduced to the vowel: Mayan (man), sayable (sable), yoyo (yo), see Af Jinni

Yarborough: without 0 or 1: 2, 3, 4, 5, 6, 7, 8, 9, 22, ...

yatsote: [Mt 5:13a acronym] "Ye are the salt of the Earth."

yawn furniture: [lawn furniture malapropism] furniture, like lounge chair, that puts one to sleep

ycpe: [Aesop acronym] "You can't please everybody."

yeen: [yellow + green portmanteau] yellow that turns to yellow, like traffic light

yesternow: [yester- back-formation] immediate past
yex: [paleologism] belch, burp, hiccough
ygologist: [mynynym back-formation] one who studies palindromes
Yksniharb's number: [Barhinsky ananym] reverse of eight-to-the-ninth-factorial, $R(8^9!)$
yod-dropped: describes a word whose long yoo phoneme changed to oo, in British English following ch, j, l, r, or sh, but in American English also following d, n, s, t, th, or z
yodded: describes a word whose short oo phoneme changed to yoo, in American English following d, n, s, t, th, or z
Yogism: [Lawrence Berra] saying of "Yogi" Berra, who said "I didn't really say half the things I said.": When you come to a fork in the road, take it. You can observe a lot by just watching. It ain't over till it's over. Always go to other people's funerals, otherwise they won't come to yours. Never answer an anonymous letter. The future ain't what it used to be. Pair up in threes. You've got to be very careful if you don't know where you are going, because you might not get there.
yoin: [Japanese] experience that continues to move interminably long after the initial external stimulus thus linking past and present, Nature and ma, artist and art-lover
yoof: [Norm Storer, euphemism] Clinton's "physical evidence", "bodily fluids", "DNA material", "forensic evidence that might suggest sexual conduct" (semen), "freedom fighters" (rebels), "collateral damage"(civilian fatalities), "friendly fire" (self-inflicted casualities), "pre-woman" (girl), "womyn" (woman)
yrumt: [grammanym] "Why are you empty?"
youmilitate: [you + humilitate portmanteau] second-hand humiliation
Young's Law: The greatest discoveries are accidental ones.
youth-in-Asia: [euthanasia mondegreen] young people in the Far East
yuefu: [Yue Fu, "music bureau"] folk-ballad tradition poems of varying line lengths, rhyme
yugen: [Japanese] awareness of creation triggering feeling too deep and mysterious for words
Zagari: describes words which change to another word when a double vowel with a z between is reduced to the vowel: bazar (bar), hazard (hard), sizing (sing), see Af Jinni
zagzig: [zigzag antonym] moving forth-and-back
zanni: [Giovanni] valet buffoon, acrobatic practical joker with common sense, intelligence, pride, but often quarrelsome, cowardly, envious, spiteful, vindictive and treacherous
zazzification: substitution of z for another consonant to turn a non-slang word into slang or make a slang word slangier, as in million to zillion
zazzooglification: [zaaification + ooglification portmanteau] turns all the consonants into z and all the vowels into oo: joycesqueanism = zoozzoozzoooooozozz
Zeitgeism: [Zeitgeist back-formation] modernism, following the latest fad
Zeitgeist: [German] prevailing mood/politics/fashions/artistic trends of a particular past era
zelda: [Matt Hudelson's Zelda] to-the-five-hundred-twelfth-two, $^{512}2$
zenaphobia: [Zena + xenophobia portmanteau] fear of women warriors
zero hour: sixty minutes following when something that isn't is or something that is isn't, see grue-bleen
zero tolerence: acceptance of a leading zero
zero problemo: confusing zero with nothing
zerone: [zero + one portmanteau] zero/one

zeugma: figure of speech in which a modifier applies in different ways to two or more words: "She opened the door and her heart to the homeless boy.", "The sky was not light, but his burden was."

zigzag: describes word alternating alphabetical direction: militarization

zilliard: [zazzified milliard] indefinite number, ten-to-the-six-z-plus-sixth, 10^{6z+6}

zillion: [zazzified million] indefinite number, ten-to-the-three-z-plus-threeth, 10^{3z+3}

Zimmerman's Law: "No one notices when things go right."

Zipf's Law: [George Kingsley Zipf] A few words are used very often, but many or most are used rarely.

ziticorumbatous: describes any 15-letter nonce word

Zivilcourage: [German] courage to express the right side of an important question that needs to be but isn't being because it's unpopular

zoo-logical: [zoological hyphenym] as logic as a sub-Human, instinctual

zoonym: [aka animalgram] zoological ananym: act (cat), alpines (spaniel), arm (ram), bare (bear), cabaret (bearcat), Californian (African lion), canter (tanrec), chained (echidna), clot (colt), corona (raccoon), crumble (clumber), emanate (manatee), ester (steer), evict (civet), flow (fowl), God (dog), gun (gnu), holed (dhole), kay (yak), leaning (eanling), lee (eel), lesions (lioness), loin (lion), love (vole), orchestra (cart horse), orange (onager), outhears (house rat), paroled (leopard), pausation (sapi outan), pelter (petrel), piratess (tarsipes), protein (pointer), rath (hart, tahr, thar), ream (mare), reed (deer), retirer (terrier), salver (serval), senators (starnose), shore (horse), someday (samoyed), tab (bat), toga (goat), trailing (ringtail), wallows (swallow), wee (ewe)

zygophrenia: personality disorder, opposite to schizophrenia, one person in two bodies, evidenced to a lesser degree in the telepathy-like twin effect

zylliard: [zazzified milliard] indefinite number, ten-to-the-six-z-plus-fourth, greater than ten billion, tenplex, $\geq 10^{10}$

zyllion: [zazzified myllion] indefinite number, ten-to-the-four-z-plus-fourth, greater than hundred million, eightplex, $\geq 10^{8}$

Zymurgy's 1st Law: Once you open a can of worms, the only way to re-can them is to use a bigger can.

zyxical: [Z, Y, X + -ical] aka zeewyexical, referring to reversed alphabet, as in words: baa, ponica, sonica, spiffed, spolia, sponged, spoofed, spooked, spooled, spoon-fe(e)d, trigged, trolled, tromba, uronic, vomica, wronged, yolked, zyxomma

zzzzzzzzzzzzzzzzzzzzzzzzzzzzzzzzzzzzzzzzzzzz: z^{43}, last word in the *Oxford English Dictionary* (as a citation)

Also from **Hierogmous Enterprises**:

All Things Are Possible: the best of Mpossibilities is a collection of articles from the newsletter of the Fortean Mysteries SIG of American Mensa.

Crosswords with Jesus is a collection of a hundred crossword puzzles that do not exclude Jesus, the Bible or the Church from *My People* newspaper.

Good News You May Have Missed in the last 30 years is a collection of articles from over thirty years of *My People* newspaper.

How to Get High is a math book based on the Proceedings of the André Joyce Appeciation Society.

The Luminous Mysteries of the Rosary is a play for 8- to 10-year-olds by Kathy McCarthy.

Psalms, Hymns and Inspired Songs is an autobiography by Michael Joseph Halm including hundreds of Scripture-inspired songs.

Proverbials: Proverbs in Verse is a collection of proverbs turned into verse by Michael Halm to bring out their poetic, memorable wisdom.

Reignbeau's Riddles and Rhymes is a collection of riddles and children' s songs by Reignbeau the Clown

Sherlock Holmes and the Mad Doctor is a science fictional/detective tale involving a certain mad doctor lost in time.

The Wizard Who Couldn't and Other Basilian Tales is a collection of fairy tales based on the Sunday Gospel readings and the history of Baselia [present day Basel region of Switzerland].

The Xoo Book, a guide to exozoology is a sampling of many strange and exotic creatures.

www.ingramcontent.com/pod-product-compliance
Lightning Source LLC
Chambersburg PA
CBHW070431290526
45791CB00005B/1920